A LEG TO STAND ON

Praise for *A Leg to Stand On*

"In the midst of adolescence, when we are all trying to figure out who we are, Colleen Haggerty literally loses a part of herself when her leg is severed in a brutal accident. In the years following, her wounded body makes it impossible to ignore a deeper wound in her spirit. Without self-pity, she confronts her own misgivings and regrets as she moves through a difficult lesson in forgiveness, both of self and others. I was engaged and cheering for her every step of the way on this courageous journey toward wholeness."

—**Hollye Dexter**, author of *Fire Season* and
co-editor of *Dancing at the Shame Prom*

"*A Leg to Stand On* is a true shero's tale, not because its author was disabled and bravely carried on but because she did something even more brave: she opened herself to the transformational power of loss. And in the way of the shero, she has brought back the details of her journey that we may share in the wisdom, growth, and grace that was hidden along the way. Yes, we see clearly here what it is to live without a leg, but more we see what it is to walk with our own becoming. That makes this book more than touching, informative, or inspiring . . . it makes it alchemical."

—**Lyena Strelkoff**, storyteller, performer, speaker, and coach

"Colleen Haggerty tells her poignant story with clarity, bravery, and a healthy respect for the depth and texture of life's choices. *A Leg to Stand On* follows a young woman's journey through crashing loss—her leg at seventeen, two abortions, two difficult pregnancies, and a long crisis of faith—to arrive at the place where she can share the truth in this courageous memoir."

—**Laura Kalpakian**, author

"In this well-written, multi-layered story, author Colleen Haggerty plays the 'honesty card' with skill, poise, and probing as she writes her way to a fuller understanding of her life. In an instant, told grippingly in the opening pages, Haggerty becomes irreversibly 'different': how she integrates this maiming into her self-identity, her sense of womanliness, partnering, and motherhood is told in such a way that her own life experience increases readers' insight into our own experience. This is the transformational magic of memoir at its best. Read if you are a woman on your own journey of understanding; read if you are a man who loves such a woman."

—**Christina Baldwin**, author of
Life's Companion: Journal Writing as a Spiritual Practice
and *Storycatcher: Making Sense of our Lives
through the Power and Practice of Story*

"Colleen Haggerty is a fierce, and mighty woman, and a force of nature. Her book—memoir—is fierce and mighty and stunning. Truthful, raw, and deeply profound, her moment of personal forgiveness will leave you breathless. I cried for her, I laughed with her, I rooted for her, and I cheered her on. I also fell in love with her all over again. This is a book about life, loss, faith, forgiveness, and love. It is also a book about awakening to the absolute greatness and beauty of our own lives."

—**Amy Ferris**, author of
Marrying George Clooney: Confessions From A Midlife Crisis

A LEG TO STAND ON

An Amputee's Walk
Into Motherhood

COLLEEN HAGGERTY

SHE WRITES PRESS

Published 2014
Printed in the United States of America
ISBN: 978-1-63152-923-8
Library of Congress Control Number: 2014943851

For information, address:
She Writes Press
1563 Solano Ave #546
Berkeley, CA 94707

In order to honor the privacy of those people who were kind enough to share their stories, the author has changed some names, places, and recognizable details.

With love and gratitude to Mark, Luke, and Tessa
for walking beside me.

PART I

• ● •

*In the midst of winter I finally learned there was
inside me an invincible summer.*

—Albert Camus

PROLOGUE

I run my fingers through the lace curtains as they flutter against my bedroom wall, and watch their shadows play with the sunbeams streaming through the window. A family of crows perches on the old fir tree outside, talking over one another in a cacophony of calls. Pots and pans clink downstairs as Mom and my two sisters make dinner.

I lie there in my bed, listening to the sounds of my own raucous family—six kids between the ages of five and thirteen. Dad and my oldest brother, Kevin, are in the yard just below my second-floor window, working on their usual Saturday afternoon project, their voices a familiar back-and-forth hum. My two youngest brothers, Matthew and David, come barreling around the corner of our well-kept colonial, their little feet slapping the concrete, yelling about some slight one did to the other. Dad's voice is placating but firm. Matt and David are always at each other. I roll my eyes, but inwardly I find their bickering somehow sweet and secure. Maybe it's because we all do it, all six of us kids. We jab at one another, literally and emotionally, always trying to rile one another up, but it is generally good-natured ribbing. We do it knowing that even if we cross the line, we'll be forgiven, no questions asked.

"Hey, Colleen!" Mom yells from downstairs. "Come set the table." I'm nine years old, and this is one of my chores this week. We all pitch in and help; we have to. Running a household of eight people takes a lot of work.

I roll over in my bed, allowing the curtains to skim my back as I get to my feet. The crows caw again, and I sense they want to talk to me. I turn back and look out the window. I make a pretty good attempt at calling back. They stop and stare at me, cock their heads. I count eight of them, just like my family. *We have the perfect family*, I think to myself. Three girls, three boys, and a mom, and a dad. I know I can't predetermine gender when I have children, but if I could have my way, I'd have the exact same family I have now: not too big, like some of the other families in our parish, and not too small. My best friend, Patty, has four kids in her family, and her house is just too quiet. I don't want quiet. I want lots of vibrant, happy energy.

I go downstairs and set the table, weaving between my sisters and Mom as they finish dinner preparations. When everyone's seated, we fold our hands in prayer and say our before-dinner blessing.

"God bless Grandma and Grandpa Pesch, Grandma and Grandpa Haggerty, all my cousins, aunts and uncles, all the priests and the sisters, the sick and the dying, and all those for whom we have promised to pray."

"*For*," Matthew says, trying not to snicker.

"Matthew, we never end a sentence with a preposition," says Dad. "It's, 'and all those *for* whom we have promised to pray.' "

Dad says this practically every night, because without fail, someone always ends that sentence with the word *for*. Often we do it just to bug him, and then we all laugh when he gives the speech *again*. If you ask me, I think he does it to play along, even though he keeps a straight face.

It's traditional, this dinner. Bowls of green beans and mashed potatoes spin around on the lazy Susan in the middle of our oval table. A plate of pot roast, a full gravy boat, and a pitcher of milk fill it out. Sometimes I get dizzy watching the food spin around as everyone takes their turn, and I have to force myself to look at my plate instead.

"Hey, Dad," says Kevin, who's eleven. "Daniel Riley said I'm on tomorrow's altar boy list. Is it okay if we go to 10:45 mass?"

"Sure, Kev."

Church is as much a part of our lives as breathing and is just as vital to our existence. God is our father in heaven, and I love him, believe in him, and want to spend my life pleasing him.

"Oh, Sharon . . . oh, this is good," Mom says to herself as she scoops up a forkful of gravy-laden mashed potatoes. Mom often compliments herself when she enjoys the dinner she's made, and it always makes me laugh inside. Whenever we have food like tonight's meal, she always says it reminds her of "home," meaning back in Minnesota where she grew up. I don't understand her nostalgia yet, but as I look around the table at everyone talking at once, I sense that this is what will be nostalgic for me: a table full of people teasing, laughing, bickering, and eating—a table full of family love.

After dinner, when the dishes are done, we all run outside for a spontaneous water fight, boys against girls, each side wielding its own hose. It's the end of a warm summer day, and we're ready to cool off. We screech with delight. I grab a bucket full of water, run around behind my dad, dump it over his head, and then run like crazy so he can't retaliate. Inside is off-limits, and our yard is big enough to accommodate the eight of us as we sneak up on one another to pounce and douse. We call it quits after everyone's drenched, and we change out of our soggy clothes in the garage. Mom scurries inside on her tiptoes to avoid leaving puddles. She's too modest to change out of her clothes in front of us. I'm not modest. I strip down along with everyone else and shiver. Our lips are turning blue as we wait for Mom to bring a tower of bath towels so we can dry off.

When it's time for bed, I go to my room. I'm the only child with her own room, and I revel in the sudden silence. I decide to leave my window open. The soft way my lace curtains move in the evening summer breeze lulls me. I snuggle against my pillow, cozy, reflecting on my perfectly normal day surrounded by my perfectly normal family. This is what I want when I'm a mom. This is what I will make happen: six kids, a perfect husband, and happy days.

I

• ● •

THE IMPACT

"I love this song," my sister Mary Beth said wistfully, as she navigated the snowy drive through the Chuckanut mountains to Bellingham, Washington. It was 1978, and the hit love song, "Sometimes When We Touch," played through the speakers of our yellow Ford station wagon. Christmas break was over, and my thirteen-year-old brother, David, and I were accompanying Mary Beth back to college, then making the two-hour drive back home to Bellevue without her. I was seventeen, and the prospect of my driving such a long stretch back thrilled me but scared me, too. Though there was still plenty of daylight left, it had begun snowing shortly after we left home almost two hours prior, and the roads up in the foothills were covered in an inch of snow.

"Yeah—I like this song, too," I said. We all started singing along, crunched together in the front seat, David sandwiched between Mary Beth and me. "I want to hold you till I die, till we both break down and cry. I want to hold you till the fear in me subsides," we bellowed at the top of our lungs.

We were creeping along at about thirty-five miles an hour with the rest of the cars, forming a serpentine as we wove through the hills.

"Oh no!" Mary Beth suddenly shouted. A white semitruck was in the left lane, and its right turn signal flicked on. It began to merge into our lane. The giant smiling face of a child eating a piece of buttered bread leered at me from the side of the semi, getting larger by the second. Mary Beth tapped gently on the brakes, but our car started to fishtail, like when I slam on my bike brakes on a bed of gravel. I threw my arm across David's stomach, like my mother would do. As the car started spinning out of control, I had this crazy memory of the teacup ride at Disneyland. My stomach dropped, and I flattened my feet against the floorboard. Though I was scared, I was also aware of how pretty the snowflakes were as they swished past the windshield. I felt like I was inside a snow globe. Then we slammed into the guardrail so hard my teeth vibrated. Our station wagon came to a stop on the left shoulder of the freeway, facing traffic. Not one of us spoke. The windshield wipers continued their lazy swiping, the radio droned on, and everything fell quiet.

The cars in the right lane kept streaming by. We sat there for what felt like ten minutes, but was probably just a minute. We all felt shaken as we watched the snow and the traffic. Obviously we needed to do something, but what?

"I'll get out and check the damage," I finally said, my voice sounding calmer than I felt. I slipped out the door and took a few steps to the front of the car, my legs trembling and my breathing shallow, to see if the tire and bumper were damaged. I felt light, like I could float away, but also relieved to get a fresh breath of cold air. Unconquerable. *We're okay!* I thought. And so was the car. I scurried back inside and made my report. We needed someone to stop traffic so we could make a U-turn. *Why isn't anyone helping?* I thought. Perhaps it was because the road conditions were dangerous enough that others didn't want to risk getting stuck. Then I wondered, *What would Kevin do?* My older brother, Kevin, was the problem-solver in the family, and since Dad's death four years ago, I always looked to him for answers. As if channeling my brother, I suddenly knew what to do. "I'll get out and flag down some help," I said. The idea made me feel proactive and smart.

I got out of the car again and walked carefully around the side and up to Mary Beth's window. She unrolled it and handed me her gloves. "Be careful," she said. David opened the passenger-side door and started to get out. "David!" she yelled. "Stay in the car!" David quickly slipped his legs back in the car and shut the door.

As soon as I was on the shoulder of the freeway, I felt foolish instead of in control. *How do I get someone to stop and help us?* I waved my arms feebly, knowing I looked stupid. Shouldn't a seventeen-year-old girl standing next to a spun-out car be an obvious call for help? What am I, *invisible*?

Just as I was about to try making eye contact with someone in a slow-moving car, I noticed a green Pacer in the left lane coming right at me. He was driving faster than the rest of the cars, too fast for how slippery I knew the road was. *You jerk*, I thought. *You're gonna spin out!*

I blinked and saw the Pacer start to skid.

There are moments in our lives that we don't—no, we *shouldn't*—remember. This was one of those moments. My world turned mercifully black. No memory was formed, at least in my conscious mind, of this one moment when the green Pacer hit my body.

Just seconds before, I was watching the car speed toward me. Then I found myself lying on the ground, my body feeling like a slab of concrete.

Mary Beth erupted out of the car. I heard her screaming. Her words were shrill and incoherent, except for, "Her leg . . . her leg . . . her leg!"

What? What about my leg? I thought. Why is she pointing *away* from me? I turned my head toward where Mary Beth was pointing, which required so much effort it surprised me, like when you're trying to run in dreams. And then I saw it. My leg. I was confused. But yes, it was my leg—far away from me, lying upside down near my waist, which didn't make sense. It was still clad in jeans and a sock. I wondered where my clog was. I looked around, but couldn't see it. *Where's my clog?* I loved my clogs. I *wanted* my clog. My body started shaking uncontrollably. *Okay*, I thought, *we need an ambulance.* I took a deep breath.

Mary Beth ran by me. *Why isn't she checking on me?* I thought.

I wanted to get her attention, but it felt impossible to talk. Instead, I heard her yelling at the man who was driving the green Pacer. His car was a few hundred yards beyond ours, and he was standing dumbly beside it. It, too, had crashed against the guardrail. "You took off her leg! Her leg came off! Look what you *did*!" she screeched hysterically. She kept screaming, but her words became fuzzy, as though I was hearing them from underwater. I heard another man gently coaxing her farther away from me in low mumbles, like when people talk in church. I heard David crying, and the man was taking David away, too. He was keeping them away from me, and I didn't know why. I wanted to scream at somebody to call an ambulance, but I didn't have the strength.

My right leg ached with a sharp intensity. It lay at a funny angle, so I tried to reposition it, but it didn't seem to obey my brain's signals, and it felt creepy to move a part of myself that felt as detached from my body as my left leg. The new position felt much worse, so I shifted it back to where it was, with effort. I was exhausted. *Where is the ambulance?*

I became distracted by my freezing crotch; it felt as though my pants were ripped open. As much as I didn't want to see the damage to my legs, I was more concerned about my crotch being exposed to the world. I summoned the courage and energy to look down, allowing my gaze to fall only as far as my crotch and no farther. I was completely covered. *Thank God.*

A young man ran up to me. His hand grasped my shoulder, firm and sure. He looked me in the eyes and said, "I'm Byron. An ambulance is on its way." I looked up into his deep-brown eyes, noticed his shock of wavy brown hair, and figured he was no older than twenty-five. My pain and fear notwithstanding, I was still a seventeen-year-old girl, and I felt a flutter of excitement being this close to such a cute guy. I later learned he was an off-duty paramedic. He started asking questions, just like they did in the TV show *Emergency.*

"What's your name?"

"Colleen."

"Colleen, how old are you?"

"Seventeen."

"Who is the president of the United States?"

"Ford."

I made the decision to stay conscious so I could continue answering his questions. I knew from *Emergency* that a conscious person makes everything easier. What I didn't know was that staying conscious would mean I'd forever remember every moment of this day and would spend decades assimilating what had happened to me.

Byron tied a tourniquet on what was left of my left leg. I moaned as it burned like a wildfire. The bottom half of my body felt inflated, huge, bloated, tight.

"Colleen, since your jacket is a pullover, I need to cut it off, so I can take your blood pressure."

My new down jacket from Eddie Bauer. I had wanted that jacket for months. It was Mom's Christmas gift to me. Knowing it was expensive made it even more special. I had owned it only nine days, and now I was watching it being cut away from my body. The small, white, downy feathers from the jacket floated lazily among the dainty little snowflakes that were falling softly from the sky. I looked at these snowflakes the way I had as a kid, when I would throw my head back to the heavens to allow them to fall onto my outstretched tongue. I was embarrassed these snowflakes were making my mascara run as they hit my eyelashes. I worried about having black mascara streaks in front of Byron.

God, I'm ugly. The thought came to me with such force that it felt physical. I had no idea how the ugliness I felt in that moment would become a central refrain in my life. All I knew was that I was ashamed. I turned away from Byron to try to pull myself together.

I craned my neck, looked behind me, and saw cars slowing down, faces pressed against windows in shocked fascination. A Greyhound bus crept by. I wanted someone to stop the bus and ask the driver to radio the hospital for an ambulance. One hadn't arrived yet, so maybe they should call again. The passengers had an aerial view of my wracked body. I knew they were trying to catch a glimpse of the person who was hit so they could tell the whole busload, with an air of superiority, what they alone had seen. My five siblings and I had done this often: creeping by the scene of an accident, we'd all stretch our necks, often our whole bodies, hoping to catch a glimpse. The lucky one could tell everyone else about the gruesome details, embellishing to his or her heart's content, until Mom's admonishment quickly stopped the narrative.

I knew they were all looking at me equally detached. I wanted to shout at them to stop staring, to leave me alone. I had never felt so exposed in my life. I looked at my chilly crotch again to be sure it was covered. It was. Good.

The need to urinate was intense. I was tempted to let my bladder loose, but I couldn't mortify myself any further by peeing on the side of the road while I lay in a bloody heap next to our car with a part of my body "over there," and a cute guy by my side.

The sound of cars driving through the crunchy snow just a few yards away couldn't drown out my sister's continued screaming. She and David were both standing about fifty feet away in the median along with the man who was taking care of them and the man who'd hit me. I must've looked pretty horrible if Mary Beth and David weren't allowed to be near me. Mary Beth slammed the driver of the Pacer with her words. "Goddamn you! You took off her leg." I saw him wrap his arms around himself, but I didn't think he was protecting himself from the cold. I wanted her to shut up. I needed quiet, but I couldn't muster the energy to tell Byron to ask her to calm down.

My thoughts start to swirl out of control. Now Mom wouldn't be able to go to Europe this spring. Now I wouldn't be in the school production of *Funny Girl*. Now Rob wouldn't like me, and we'd never get together. Now I wouldn't be able to go to college . . .

I wanted to hold on to something. I reached for Byron's hand. My legs hurt so much, like they were on fire. I wanted to break down and cry, but I couldn't. I knew that if I started to cry, all that emotion would get caught in my throat and my head would explode from my body, just like my leg had. So I couldn't break down. I had to hold on until the ambulance got there. I squeezed Byron's hand, but then I realized I was squeezing too hard. I loosened my grip, but still, I held on. I held on. He squeezed my hand back.

The faint sounds of the siren gradually increased as the ambulance finally approached. *It's coming*, I thought. *I'll be okay.* I became confused when the sound started to recede. *Don't they know where I am? Is it for someone else?* My eyes reached Byron's and asked the question.

"The ambulance has to go south on the freeway, exit, then come north to where we are. But because of the snowy conditions, it has to go slow," Byron explained. "Hang in there, Colleen."

I knew getting to the hospital was vital. In *Emergency*, the ambulance always arrives at the scene quickly—but this was taking so long. I fought off sleep while I waited, knowing it was important to stay awake to answer any questions the ambulance drivers would have.

When the ambulance finally arrived, the paramedics scurried out carrying their portable phone—just like on *Emergency*. This, I thought, was a story to tell my younger brothers, who liked watching the show as much as I did. I started to relax as I heard Byron talking to one of the paramedics. I looked to my left and saw the other paramedic pick up and cradle the remains of my leg. I was surprised and touched by how gently he held it, as if he were holding a baby. *Is he going to throw it away in an ordinary garbage can, or do they have special garbage cans for dismembered body parts?* I wanted to say good-bye to my leg, but I didn't want to appear stupid.

"Hi, Colleen, we're going to get you to the hospital. We need to get you in the ambulance, so we'll slide you onto our bed," the paramedic explained. Though they slid me effortlessly onto the ambulance bed on the count of three, every inch of my body from the stomach down joined my voice in painful screams. They rolled me into the truck. I looked around, amazed at how lifelike the show really was. I'd seen the inside of this ambulance on TV every week. Its chrome walls were so clean they looked like a mirror. All the supplies were neatly stacked against the walls, and the bed fit on the left side of the bay. There was room next to the bed for one of the paramedics to sit next to me. I knew he would need to monitor my vitals.

I glimpsed my sister as she ran to our car and fetched my book bag, another Christmas gift. Then I heard her voice in the front seat of the ambulance next to the driver. David tentatively stepped up into the back of the ambulance next to me. I attempted to smile at him, but he wasn't looking at me—he was looking for a place to sit. The other paramedic, the one taking care of me, cleared a spot for David.

The paramedic poked a needle into my arm while the driver called us in over the radio, "St. Luke's, we're coming in."

I knew I could let go and sleep. I shut my eyes, but they snapped open as I realized I hadn't yet prayed. *How can I have gone this long without a prayer?* I had been attending mass every day before school. My relationship with God was intact and strong, wasn't it? Guiltily, I wondered why prayer wasn't my first act.

The ambulance doors banged shut, and I began: *Hail Mary, full of grace, the Lord is with thee. Blessed art thou among women and blessed is the fruit of thy womb, Jesus. Holy Mary, Mother of God, pray for us sinners now and at the hour of our death. Amen.*

2

• ● •

SEPARATION AND ISOLATION

My eyes popped open, but it was still dark. The hospital was cold and quiet save for the distant hum of this huge edifice working around the clock. Flowers packed the room, masking the antiseptic odor. I didn't need to look at the clock; I knew what time it was. For the last week, I'd woken up every morning at three a.m., my body needing its next fix of pain medication, which I still insisted be given by injection instead of orally. The act of taking a pill—putting it in my mouth, holding a cup of water, and swallowing—required too much effort.

I lay with my arms bent at the elbow, my hands resting palms-up beside my ears as if in surrender. I couldn't sleep any other way. The cast dug painfully into my crotch, and any attempt to readjust my position served as a nauseating reminder of my missing leg. It was unnatural and disturbing how nearly weightless my abbreviated leg felt now. The doctors told me I'd lost about twelve pounds of leg. I was reminded of how I'd felt after taking a long hike while carrying a fifty-pound backpack. Upon reaching camp, I'd take off the pack and walk around, reacquainting myself with the sudden lightness of my own body—yet feeling it was missing something, so familiar had I become with the extra weight.

I looked out the window toward the Space Needle, still decorated with Christmas lights. Christmas, the day of Jesus's birth. For the first time in my life, I felt a twinge of uncertainty and doubt about my faith. The story of Christ's salvation had sustained and comforted me during even the hardest of times—my father's death. But now I felt betrayed by God. I'd spent my life being the "good girl." I was reliable, I was responsible, and, for the past six months, I'd gone to mass every day before school with my mom. I loved Jesus, I praised God, and I adored Mary. My reward for my goodness would come later, I'd been promised—it would come. But this was no reward. Doubt's door had been opened.

As I lay silent and still in the midst of this new dark doubt, I struggled to understand why this might have happened to me. Up to that point, my only framework for making sense of difficult things came from my youthful faith in cause and effect. If I did right, God would do right by me. Was this accident God's message to me about something I had done?

Perhaps I'm being punished! I thought, feeling a tight panic. *For what, though?* There was a boy in my choir class who had a deformed hand. When I first noticed it, my stomach lurched, and I had to keep the bile from exploding from my mouth. I couldn't bring myself to sit next to him, let alone talk to him. Whenever I found myself near him, I was certain his deformed hand smelled like a garbage dump on a summer's day. Was God punishing me for being disgusted by that boy's deformity by making me deformed, too? Somehow, the punishment didn't seem to fit the crime, but what other reason could God have for doing this to me?

The ache I felt in my heart now was worse than the one I'd felt after Dad's sudden death four years earlier, when he had drowned in a boating accident. The pain and shock I'd felt then was placated by assurances that it was simply "Dad's time to go"—that "God wanted Dad with him." My faith assured me that my relationship with Dad was not over, it was merely changed: he was now my personal angel. After his death, I talked to him every night before sleep. I needed to believe he was still with me, or I wouldn't survive my sadness. Thus, although I missed him terribly, my life carried on without him, my faith in his altered existence intact. But this felt different. How could my life possibly go on now, with a part of *myself* missing?

I wasn't ready for the fact that there are some things faith can't explain. But here I was, ready or not.

I hadn't been ready six days ago, either, when on the day after the accident, while I lay in the intensive-care unit, groggy and in shock, Mom read me my acceptance letter to my first-choice university. The relief in her voice was palpable. In my medicated daze, I mimicked her smile. Nor was I ready a few days later, when my drama teacher visited me in the hospital and handed me my script for *Funny Girl*. On the last day of school before Christmas break, I had quickly scanned the casting list posted in the hallway near the drama department. Next to "Mrs. Strakosh" was my name! I'd spent the break thrilled that I landed a singing role in a musical. I didn't expect to still be in the play, which was just two and a half months away. But there she sat, smiling, eyes determined, like she was doing me a favor. Didn't they realize everything had changed? How could they expect so much from me? College? Acting? The accident, with its terrible cost, had ripped something more from me than half my leg; it had torn a hole in the fabric of my being. I felt frayed around the edges. Why did God do this to me? How could I go on with life—be the overachiever I was expected to be—when I was mad as hell and doubting everything I'd ever believed in?

I'd have to find a way, because my situation wasn't going to change.

I turned my gaze down at my stump. Yes, this is what it was called, like having a new body part altogether. Only those of us with appendages that have been whacked off, like a fallen tree, get the honor of using this ugly term to describe a part of our body. I was reminded of the tree stump outside the kitchen window at home. I was told Native Americans had cleared our land, and in our family's view, this stump was a prized reminder of their existence before our arrival. Now I felt a kinship with the lost tree. I wondered if it had been as painful for the tree to be whacked by an axe as it had been for me to be hit by a car. The tree stump was camouflaged by salal, so it was actually pretty now. My stump would never be pretty.

The small lump under the white blanket ended too quickly. The small lump, enclosed in rolls and rolls of casting material to keep the swelling down, was too wide. The small lump made me sick. I quickly turned my eyes away.

I'd never thought I was pretty. I was a pear-shaped girl with small breasts and a big butt, which I jokingly referred to as my "child-bearing hips." Attempts to find a cute hairstyle always failed me; my straight, shoulder-length red hair would quickly lose body in the damp Seattle weather. My defining feature was my vibrant blue eyes, and people often commented on how they sparkled. But I knew sparkling eyes couldn't carry me through life, now that I had lost a part of my body. Any feeble fantasies I'd had about developing long, sexy legs were dashed. Now I wouldn't be wearing the fashionable hot pants. High heels were out of the question. My physical therapist would later inform me that freckles could be added to my prosthetic leg to match my other leg. She'd laughed when she said this. Was she being funny? I couldn't tell, so I had laughed along anyway.

But freckles were only part of what would be needed to make a prosthetic leg look natural on me. In fourth grade, I had to give an oral report in front of the class. I was wearing my school uniform: a plaid skirt and a white blouse. In the middle of my report, I looked up and saw the two popular girls pointing at me and laughing. I searched out my best friend Patty and looked at her beseechingly. She pointed to my legs. I looked down and saw the purple veins, like the roots of a tree, climbing down my thighs. I was so white and so cold that the veins showed through like my skin was tissue paper. With teary eyes, I looked to my teacher to make them stop laughing. She flicked her hand swiftly at me instead, as if to say, "Continue." Could the prosthetist replicate purple veins, too?

Every night I was haunted by thoughts of God, normality, beauty, and what my future could possibly look like with only one leg. Everything I'd ever imagined for my life was slipping away, and I needed some kind of control, some sense of choice in all that was happening. I finally made a decision that gave me just the tiniest feeling that my life belonged to me—that it was not God's to play with anymore. I kept the decision to myself at first, but knew I would need to say it out loud sooner or later.

One day, Mom was looking out the window of my hospital room, which overlooked the steeples of the nearby Catholic church. The gray January light streamed through the window, filling the room with the same heaviness that rested in my heart. She turned and looked at me with a mixture of sorrow, strength, and pain in her eyes. They told me I could tell her my thoughts and I wouldn't be admonished.

"Mom," I said, tentatively, "I need to talk to you." She came over, sat near my bed, and held my hand. Dad's death had been so hard for her to bear. I didn't want to add to her pain, but I had to tell her the thoughts I had been plagued by since the accident—and tell her about my decision.

"What is it, honey?"

"Mom," I told her, "I think you should know I've decided to have sex before I get married." Now, I was quite proud of my Catholic upbringing and my good-girl status, so this wasn't something I took lightly. At my public high school, I gallantly referred to myself as "Colleen Wait-Until-Wedding-Night Haggerty." Everyone, including myself, laughed when I said this, but we all knew I meant it; there'd never been any confusion about my stance on premarital sex.

I didn't know a lot about sex. I had only kissed a few boys and still considered kissing, especially French kissing, a bit gross. But I knew enough to know I would be naked during sex. I knew legs wrapped around bodies in moments of passion, and I'd have only one leg to do the wrapping.

"My future husband needs to know what he's getting into. It's only fair to let him see me and know what having sex with me will be like, so he'll know if he'll be grossed out."

Mom quietly nodded her head and said, "Okay." This only

confirmed I was right to think men would be repulsed by me. But something deeper nagged at me, a thought that was hard to acknowledge, let alone admit to my mother: I was terrified that my family dream was shattered. I'd built a fleshed-out fantasy of my life as a mother to a happy brood of redheaded children, married to a kind and funny man, living a life of beautiful chaos, not too dissimilar from my own. Marriage, motherhood, babies, children—this seemed suddenly as remote a possibility as getting my leg back. *Who would ever want to make love to me now?* I wondered, desolate.

My mother's one-word answer, her "okay" in the face of my announcement, spoke to an affirmation that the life I'd counted on was going to be out of my reach. Maybe if she'd argued with me, or even shamed me for my decision to forego virginity before marriage, I would have known she hadn't discarded the dream for my life we had both shared. But she didn't fight for that dream, and so neither would I.

In the fantasy future I'd spun, there was only one boy I'd ever imagined playing the part of husband and father: Rob. When I met him my sophomore year of high school, my heart melted to my knees. He was a boy of medium build, with piercing dark-brown eyes, a sharp nose, and high cheekbones. His silky brown hair, cut in the fashionable Bruce Jenner style, looked so soft that I wanted to touch it. He had a jolly kind of walk, causal and carefree. There wasn't a macho bone in his body.

He was a year ahead of me in school, and my crush on him was hard to hide. We were both involved in the drama department, so there was plenty of opportunity to be around him. While we never spent time alone together outside of school, I occasionally found myself alone with him while working on a drama project. I giggled nervously and laughed too loud at his jokes, all the while trying to hide my feelings for him and the nervousness I felt just being around him.

I shared my feelings with only a few close friends. This was more than a mere crush, and I wanted to protect myself. I had seen too many people in high school confide their secrets and then have others walk all over them. I thought I'd die if anyone trampled over my precious feelings for Rob. My few close friends encouraged me to ask Rob to the Sadie Hawkins dance my junior year. It took days for me to build up the gumption. A week before the dance, I found him alone near his locker after school. Without a greeting, I just blurted it out. "Rob, will you go to the Sadie Hawkins with me?" He was so excited, he jumped up and down in the hallway. I blushed, smiled, and my heart leapt. Memories of the dance were a blur, but I did remember the electric feeling of his body close to mine as we slow-danced, and I wondered if he felt it, too.

But he never asked me out on a date after the dance, so I assumed he just wanted to be friends. Though disappointed, I liked him so much I wanted to be his friend, which was enough.

Rob graduated at the end of my junior year and attended the local community college the next fall. Without him at school, my feelings lay dormant. Occasionally, I saw him at weekend parties, stoking the smoldering fire in my heart. But he never called me, so I eventually stopped fantasizing about him and focused instead on my senior-year activities. The promise of him now was even more remote, but after the accident, he rose in my thoughts again, like crocuses returning in the spring.

When my friends visited me in the hospital one afternoon soon after my talk with my mom, I wanted to ask if they knew whether or not Rob had heard of the accident. But I was tongue-tied, and simply seeing them made me feel awkward and distant. I noticed how they forced themselves to look at my face, and I could sense their morbid curiosity to look at the remainder of my leg, the small bump hidden under the bedcovers.

"Did you hear about Jack and Amy?" Brandy asked. Brandy and I had been friends since sophomore year, when we'd met in our first play together. "They broke up!"

Sarah, whom I also knew from the drama department, chimed in, "I heard Jack is really bummed about it, but Amy acts like she doesn't care." Jack and Amy were the golden couple of the senior class. I listened as they reported on the couple's latest crisis, but high school news now seemed trivial and meaningless. Their words sounded like the schoolteacher in the Charlie Brown comics: "*Wah, wah, wah, wah, wah.*" I smiled, nodded my head, and laughed when they laughed, but I felt as disconnected from them as my leg was from my body.

As I lay in my hospital bed the night after my friends' visit, frustrated and forlorn, I wept, feeling so separate from the people who had become my second family. Gail, a kind nurse, heard me whimpering and came into my room. "I'll listen," she said softly.

"They all feel so far away and in another world. They don't understand what I'm going through." She explained they were all too immature for me now and they couldn't understand. This didn't help. I didn't want to be mature. I didn't want to be in the position where my friends needed to "understand" me. That was for grownups. I just wanted to be a senior in high school.

My father's death, which happened while I was in junior high school, had thrown me into the "other" category. "Oh, she's the one whose dad drowned." Few students talked to me about his death, and when they did, they asked questions about the accident, not about how I was feeling. I quickly learned that my feelings, precious and deep, had to be kept to myself. Now here I was again, thrown into the "other" category. I knew all too well how to mask my emotions. But I could already tell this wasn't going to be like Dad's death. This was too integral to who I was. Masking my feelings while I dealt with what was on the horizon for me was going to take extra effort.

I turned my gaze to the lit Christmas tree on the top of the Space Needle and said what would be my last prayer for a long time. "You weren't supposed to do this to me. I have worked so hard to be good, and this is how you treat me. If that's how you're going to play, fine. But don't expect adoration and blind faith any longer. I'll do everything I can to deal with this, and you do everything you can to help me." It wasn't a deal or an ultimatum. It was my last stand. This was cruel. This was unfair. This was like a sinister prank. And God isn't supposed to be evil. All the rules had changed. I didn't know how yet, but I'd figure out the new rules and beat this game somehow. I knew I still needed God's help; I just wasn't going to ask for it again. He didn't deserve my respect. Because of what he did to me, he had to take responsibility for helping me handle this.

I turned my head away from the window, pushed the button on my call light, and waited for the nurse to arrive with the next injection.

3

ATTA GIRL

Mom was tidying my hospital room in the same way she tidied the living room at home. She called it "putzing." She stacked all the get-well cards neatly on the bedside table, freshened the water in the many bouquets of flowers, and picked up the stray magazines strewn about the room. I was lying in bed, tired, thinking about my friends living the life I had been living just a week ago. I missed them, but because I couldn't relate to them anymore, I was so lonely.

My thoughts were suddenly interrupted by loud clapping coming from the doorway. "Time to get you up!" A stocky, strong-looking woman with short, sandy-blonde hair walked in. She was wearing khaki pants, a white shirt, and a big smile. "Hi! I'm Anne, your physical therapist, and we're going to get you vertical today."

I was baffled. It had only been a week since the accident. I looked at Mom, who was looking in her compact mirror as she applied a fresh coat of lipstick. I could tell from her reassuring smile that she had been apprised of this new development. Anne maneuvered a gurney to the side of my bed. Clearly, I had no choice in the matter, and Anne's practiced, no-nonsense demeanor assured me she had done this before.

She and a nurse transferred me to the gurney by sliding me—using the sheet I was lying on—and then wheeled me out into the hall in the direction of what I would soon understand was the physical therapy department. I hadn't been outside my room yet, and my nose was assaulted by the antiseptic odor, which had been pretty well masked in my room by the fresh bouquets of flowers. "Good luck, Colleen," I heard from the staff behind the nursing station desk. I glanced at them and attempted a smile as we glided past—and realized I didn't even recognize all of them. A young nurse I hadn't seen before waved at me. *How do they know my name?* As Anne pushed me down the wide hallway and chatted with Mom, I noticed my hands were sweaty. I was starting to get nervous. What was physical therapy going to be like? What was Anne going to expect from me? In an effort to allay my fears, I looked into the patient rooms as we passed. Most of the patients I glimpsed were old, curled in their beds, moaning or sleeping. I felt so sad for them.

When we reached the physical therapy department, I felt the buzz of activity. The high-ceilinged room was full of patients doing exercises on elevated blue mats. Large picture windows lined one wall, allowing the sun to stream in. Anne pushed me to one side of the room and slid my gurney perpendicular to the wall. She and one of her female aides slid me onto a padded platform about six feet long—called a "tilt table"—and strapped me in across my torso.

"Okay, time for the ride of your life!" Anne said, smiling. She pushed a button, and the table slowly hummed its way to a forty-five-degree angle. I held on for dear life. I hadn't been vertical in a week—a week in which each day held an eternity.

"Okay, how do you feel?" she asked.

"Nervous," I said. But actually, I felt great. I felt tall. I felt like I had regained a little of myself by not looking at the world from a bed.

"Okay, then we'll go higher." The table continued its slow rotation to ninety degrees. "How's this?"

"Fine?" I said. Anne was clearly pleased, and she and Mom talked about how unusual it was for someone in my situation to do so well at ninety degrees. I knew this was a small thing, but I was proud of myself. "Well, champ, that's all for now. We don't want to tax your delicate constitution," she said with a wink.

"I'm done?" I was surprised—and relieved nothing more was expected of me.

"Oh, no, you can't get rid of me so easily. I'll see you again this afternoon at three o'clock. That will be our schedule every day: eleven in the morning and three in the afternoon."

I was napping and Mom was reading a magazine when Anne strode into my room at three o'clock, grinning like the Cheshire cat. "Good afternoon! Are you ready for round two?"

During this session, instead of sliding me onto a gurney, she talked me through how to sit up, turn my body, and transfer myself into a wheelchair. Her arms were around me, guiding me through each step, her breath warm on my neck. She gave off the clean scent of soap and shampoo. Every movement felt awkward and unsettling. The weight differential between my legs was significant. I just wanted to lie back down and go to sleep. I wanted to escape this reality. But Mom was squealing with delight. "Oh, look, honey, you're sitting up!"

"How do you feel? Are you dizzy?" Anne's question and Mom's delight helped me settle into the chair, into the room, into my body.

"No, I'm not dizzy. I feel okay."

Anne sat down in a chair across from me, and while she focused on cleaning her fingernails, one nail under the other, she asked me where I went to school, what grade I was in, and what I did after school. Mom sat in the background, flipping the pages of a magazine. After I had answered her questions, Anne said, "Okay, then!" and stood up.

"Your job today is to sit in this chair until you're tired, hopefully through dinner—if you can eat it," she said with a twinkle in her eye. I hadn't eaten solid food in a week so regardless of what dinner tasted like, I would eat it.

Mom had to go home to tend to my brothers at dinnertime, so I was alone when Gail, the nurse who'd talked to me about my friends, delivered my dinner. She took the warming top off the plate with a flourish, her arm sweeping the air. "Ta-da, steak and potatoes! It's actually pretty good. Eat as much as you can, but don't overdo it."

"Okay," I said as she left the room. I suddenly felt so alone, which I was used to, but this was a weird alone. I felt like a stranger to myself. I was used to spending a lot of solitary time out in the woods behind our house, walking the mazelike trails, but now I wasn't quite sure of who I was—and this made me feel panicky when no one else was in the room with me. I nibbled at the steak. It was juicy but too hard to swallow—though harder to swallow still was the fact that I had to figure out who I was. At least Anne saw me as someone who was trying to heal, but that wasn't much of an identity. I ate about half my dinner before despair made me too tired to finish.

The next day, Anne showed me exercises to help me regain my strength. Except for gym class, I had rarely exercised on purpose. My athletic inexperience coupled with my injury made me feel very awkward and self-conscious while I was doing exercises that required me to lift my remaining full leg, which the doctors had saved with some effort, up in the air.

"Ah, come on, I know you're stronger than that," she said, which challenged me to lift my leg higher. "You can do five more, trust me." I squeezed out five more painful leg lifts. "There. What did I tell you? You're stronger than my horses at home," she said with a laugh that echoed throughout the room. I left therapy feeling surprisingly strong and confident.

On the third day, Anne attached a round metal pylon to the bottom of the cast covering my residual leg. The pylon was about two inches in circumference and looked like a pipe. As she anchored it in place, she explained how I was going to walk. But I was only half listening. I didn't want to hear what she was saying. I looked away, not wanting to see the replacement for the part of me I hadn't yet let go of, not wanting her to see the tears well up in my eyes. She gripped my arm and said, "Hey, you're gonna do great." Her smile was infectious, and so was her attitude. She hardly knew me and yet was so sure I'd succeed. I felt like I was riding piggyback. So I swallowed my grief, put a smile on my face, and decided to live up to Anne's confidence in me.

Anne rolled my wheelchair to the parallel bars and applied the brakes. She used the therapy belt buckled around my waist to lift me from the chair. For the first time since the accident, I was standing. I felt unbalanced, which was disorienting, so I grabbed the parallel bars on either side of me and held on tightly. I didn't want to look down and see my missing leg, so I raised my head, but at the end of the parallel bars was a full-length mirror. I couldn't believe what I saw. Was that was actually me? Blue-and-white hospital gown. Straight, greasy hair. Pale, white skin. Big bandage on my right leg. Metal for my left. I wanted to run away and sob until I couldn't feel anything anymore, but Anne was there, bellowing out orders. "Bear weight on your arms and lift your left leg." I was disoriented, because the pylon—my left leg—was nearly weightless. I looked around the room for something to concentrate on besides the mirror.

"Good. Now move that leg forward and set 'er down," she ordered. I did. "See, you just took your first step!" she said encouragingly. "Now let's try the right side."

I took a step with my right leg. Anne held the belt around my torso, tightly at first, then she slowly loosened her grip. I focused on her hands, strong with short, dirty fingernails. I held on to the bars, bearing more and more of my own weight. She didn't coo her praise; she barked it. "Good! Take another step. Great! Hey, would you look at this everyone? She's walking!"

I heard people clapping. I started to giggle. Sweat dripped into my eyes and down my sides, but I couldn't take my arms off the bars to wipe it away. Yes, people were looking at me as I hobbled around in a stupid hospital gown with a pylon for a leg. I was sweating like a pig, and my hair looked like crap. But I was *walking*. For the first time since the accident, I felt hopeful. Perhaps I wouldn't lie in bed for the rest of my life. Perhaps I would walk again. Perhaps there was an identity to build for myself as someone who could overcome her circumstances. I reached the end of the bars and saw that some-one had moved my wheelchair there. Anne helped me sit down, and I rested. I had walked ten feet and was exhausted. Anne slapped me on the back, and I laughed through my tears.

"You ready to walk back?" she asked.

"No," I said, laughing, feeling both elated and exhausted. "But I will." I liked Anne, and I wanted to please her.

Anne helped me stand up. I grabbed the parallel bars and slowly walked to the other end. Anne narrated the entire walk. "That's right, now pick up the right foot. Don't you wish walking had been this easy when you were a baby? Now the left . . . Good, good! Just a few more steps and you're there. Atta girl, you're an old pro."

4

AT LAST

Anne's confidence and commanding spirit held me in place during the rest of my stay in the hospital. When I said good-bye to her and the rest of the staff, I felt ready to go home and resume my life. But that readiness was short-lived.

Mom pulled up to the hospital door in her small hatchback and I had a new hurdle to cross: getting into a car again. I choked back the tears as I struggled to fit my crutches into the backseat. I was afraid to get in. *What if we get hit on the way home?* I thought as I plopped myself onto the passenger seat. I could hardly breathe as Mom drove, especially as she navigated through rush-hour traffic. Every time a car passed us, I wrung my hands and closed my eyes, but behind my lids I could see that green Pacer speeding toward me.

We pulled into our driveway and parked behind an unfamiliar car. My stomach sank. I didn't want any visitors right then. But then Mary Beth opened the front door and came out of the house, her eyes gleaming with tears. Mary Beth had bought a used car so she could easily commute between college and home to see me on the weekends. She had been to see me at the hospital, but she had classes to attend in Bellingham, so I hadn't seen her in a week. I was overjoyed to see her, but I also thought I saw guilt in her eyes as I hobbled toward her. My heart swelled with love and a desire to comfort her. *She has nothing to feel guilty about. It's all his fault, the guy who was driving the Pacer*, I thought. But I didn't say anything.

I simply stood in front of her, willing her to be okay and hoping that someday, when we were both ready, we'd have a chance to talk about it.

After dinner with the family and a TV show with Mary Beth, I was ready for bed. My bedroom was on the second floor, up a flight of thirteen stairs. Standing at the bottom and looking up to the top of the staircase was like looking up to the top of Mt. Rainier.

"Do you need any help?" Mary Beth asked. The desperate helplessness in her voice made me want to protect her from her own feelings. *The quicker I recover, the better everyone else will feel,* I thought. Aside from carrying me up the stairs, there was nothing she could do. I was on my own with this task.

"No thanks, I got it," I said. I took a deep breath and crutched up the first step. By the time I got to the top, I was sweating from exertion, almost too tired to crutch down the hallway to my bedroom. Mary Beth, who had followed me up, gave me a tight hug good night and then I made my way down to my room. When I opened the door, I couldn't go in right away. I felt the absence of my leg in a new way. I looked at my bed. The last time I'd crawled into that bed, I had two legs. I gazed at my desk. The last time I studied at that desk, I crossed my now-missing left leg over my right leg.

I noticed a pair of my jeans folded over my chair. The last time I wore those jeans, I'd slipped *both* legs into them. I remembered how rushed I had been the morning I last left this bedroom, scurrying on my capable two legs to get out the door. Little did I know how much my life would change that day.

Finally, I took a breath and stepped into my room. I thought that at least in here, the room that had always been my refuge—particularly there in the bed where I talked to Dad every night before sleep—I could sort through the feelings that had been taunting me in the middle of the night at the hospital. I was still on pain medication, but not a high dose, so perhaps I could think more clearly now in the safety of my own space.

Unfortunately, as soon as I managed to take off my pylon and climb into bed, a flood of thoughts and fears came crashing down on me. What was I going to do now? Go back to school and act normal? Would I be able to go to college? Get a job? Would I need Mom's physical and financial help the rest of my life? How would I make money and provide for myself? All of my classmates were planning their futures with an air of hope and expectancy. I would be planning mine with heavy feelings of doubt and dread. I had already convinced myself that I was far too ugly now to ever have a normal relationship with a man. Was I even going to be able to look people in the eye? Especially the boys? Can a girl with one leg flirt with a boy? I didn't know what the new rules would be for me.

Thinking about all of this was not a good idea after all. It was just going to drive me crazy. There was nothing I could do about it. Nothing. I leaned back against my pillows and closed my eyes. My life was out of my control. In my exhaustion, I started to drift off to sleep. And then out of the blue came the scene of the accident. The cold of snow falling on my face. The sound of traffic passing by. The green Pacer coming at me. I awoke to my own gasp just as the car was about to hit me. Why didn't that stupid jerk slow down?

With my eyes now wide open, I looked around the room for something to anchor me. Jeans on the chair. My desk. The door that led to the hallway and to the rest of my family. And I wondered if he even knew my name or what had become of me. I'd heard his name was Harvey. The church had said we should pray for our enemies, but I wasn't talking to God anymore, and I certainly wasn't going to pray for the man who ruined my life. Tears sprang to my eyes as my anger intensified.

"Colleen, are you already in bed?" Mom called as she walked in to check on me. "Do you need anything?"

I took another breath and turned my attention to her smile. "No thanks, Mom." I knew she wanted to tend to my immediate needs, but what I needed right then was for her to answer my growing list of questions about how I was supposed to move forward. I knew, though, I just knew, she didn't have the answers. "I'm fine. Good night."

A few days after I returned home, Mom asked the therapist she'd been seeing the past few years to make a house call to see me. I was conflicted about this. On the one hand, I was nervous about talking to someone I didn't know. In my naïveté, I was afraid he'd somehow hypnotize me and force me to bare my soul, exposing all the private thoughts that had been swirling around since the accident. On the other hand, I was hopeful that there might be someone with an answer to all my questions about who I was supposed to be now.

Mom walked Mr. Riggs into the family room where I was waiting for him. After introductions, Mom left us alone. She shut the family room door behind her. I heard the muffled sounds as she spoke to my brothers in the kitchen next door.

I never had the chance to find out what would have happened if I'd opened up to Mr. Riggs. He spent most of his hour with me talking about a friend of his who lost his leg in a motorcycle accident—and assuring me that I'd be fine.

"Don't worry about a thing," he said at one point.

How could he say that? Things were not going to be fine. If I had two legs, everything would be fine, but I didn't. *That's why he's here, isn't it?*

I didn't know much about therapy, but I knew the therapist wasn't supposed to do most of the talking. Like my friends who visited me in the hospital, I sensed his discomfort with me. I stopped listening to him after fifteen minutes and decided that, if a therapist couldn't handle my feelings, I'd have to rely on myself to deal with my amputation and my future.

The following week, I was sitting on the living room floor reading a book after dinner. Mom sat on the couch, with the coffee table in between us. She interrupted my focus by placing a few pieces of paper on the table. I glanced at the papers and then looked up at her. Her eyebrows were raised—not in a question, but in expectation.

"What's this?" I asked.

"This is a list of everyone who helped out while you were in the hospital, people who sent flowers and did nice things. You need to write thank-you notes to these people." She pushed the list across the table to me.

I stared numbly at the list of nearly fifty names. Beads of sweat started to form on my brow, and I felt tears forming in my eyes. She wanted me to write thank-you notes? What I could possibly say to these people? I couldn't imagine writing the words "thank you" fifty times after what I had been through. Thank you? Thank you for what? Thanks for sending flowers after I lost my leg? Thanks for sending over a casserole after I lost my leg? This wasn't like a birthday or Christmas.

My agitation increased as Mom kept her eyebrows arched in that "do as I'm telling you" expression. I was dumbfounded. Shouldn't people be writing notes to me? I'm the one who lay on the side of the road and watched my leg be carried away by a paramedic. I'm the one who endured hours of physical therapy, sweat dripping down my entire body, as I learned to walk again. Thank-you notes? I couldn't believe she was asking me to do this, but I didn't have the wherewithal to challenge her. Challenging my mother wasn't what I did, and I wasn't about to start now.

So I took the list from her and dutifully wrote each and every thank-you note. I wrote "Thank You" again and again and again. While I was being the obedient daughter I had always been, I did so secretly resenting each word I wrote—and my own quiet compliance.

After taking a lot of time off from work, Mom needed to return. She arranged for her friends to take turns checking in on me while she was at the office. I knew these women since they were all from church and bridge buddies of Mom's, but I felt awkward spending time alone with them. And then the perfect distraction arrived.

One afternoon while I was still recuperating, Rob called to ask if he could visit. I spent an hour fixing my hair and finding something to wear to hide the pylon as much as possible. With the feeling of an Alka-Seltzer tablet exploding in my stomach, I worried I might actually throw up from the excitement of seeing him again. I had been barraged with visitors, but no one made my skin tingle or made me forget my heartache like Rob did when he walked in our front door. He came at about four in the afternoon, and we spent the next two hours talking nonstop. All my old feelings surfaced as I caught a whiff of his scent and watched his eyes glisten as he laughed. That was the first normal conversation I had had with someone outside my family since the accident. Rob and I talked like old friends, picking up from where we had left off when he graduated last spring. With my other friends, the conversation was steered around the elephant in the room; with Rob, the elephant didn't exist. I found myself laughing too loudly as he did his impressions of different Monty Python characters with an exaggerated British accent and his face drawn like an old butler. He ended up staying through dinner and watching TV with the family afterward, and then we talked some more, sitting on the living room floor in front of the fire. Our conversation turned more serious as he talked about how my accident had affected him.

"Colleen, when I heard about your accident and how you could have died, it was a wake-up call. I realized I have feelings for you, and now is my opportunity to let you know how I feel. I don't want to let this moment pass."

My face flushed. Fears that I could never be loved as an amputee came forward, but I pushed them away. I looked up at him, not knowing what to say.

"I have to ask. Do you share these feelings toward me?"

I laughed and exhaled my pent-up angst and disappointment.

"Yes, Rob, I do. Actually, I have for a long time." After years of keeping my feelings for Rob a secret, I felt like I was betraying myself by uttering those words. But I knew I had to admit my feelings to him in order to propel this conversation forward. And I so much needed this to happen.

"Well, then," he said, very formally, "I'd like to ask if you will be my girlfriend." His eyes squinted in anticipation of my answer. My own eyes popped open in surprise and elation.

"Really?" I squeaked. This was happening so fast. Did he mean it? But looking into his hopeful face, I could see this wasn't a mean joke. I took a deep breath before I said yes.

We were sitting on the floor, and I was still figuring out how to maneuver my body with the cast and the pylon, so our hug was awkward. We stood up, and he looked deep into my eyes. "May I kiss you?"

All I could do was nod my head.

I didn't know or understand what swooning was until I kissed Rob that night. I felt like the earth had completely disintegrated, and I was floating in a sea of happiness. The doubt and anger I had experienced during the past three weeks seemed to vanish. A simple kiss and a warm, generous hug from the boy I had liked for so long made me hope I could set aside the ugliness of my self-hatred and the fear of the future.

In three short weeks, I'd been initiated into an extreme range of emotions. The despair and pain my heart could tolerate shocked me. From day to day, I could hardly understand, let alone name, what I was feeling. And then, in one moment, the knot of sadness was replaced by the beauty and joy now filling my heart. But, love notwithstanding, I couldn't escape the sobering facts that I still needed a prosthetic leg, I still needed physical therapy, and I still needed to learn to walk without crutches. At least, I told myself, I had Rob, the boy of my dreams, by my side to help me weather all that was ahead.

5

• ● •

A NEW PART

As I emerged from the accident, I learned there was more to recovery than focusing on my own healing. There was a world of people out there I had to consider—all who had their thoughts about who I should become. Two years of high school drama paid off well. I already had the skills to portray myself on the outside as something completely different from how I felt on the inside. I was also quickly figuring out how to align myself with other people's expectations.

When I was home recuperating after my hospital stay, one of Mom's friends gave me a copy of *Reader's Digest* with a page dog-eared, pointing to an article about an amputee who had scaled a mountain. In an attempt to give me hope, many people had begun to relay such stories to me of amputees they knew or heard about who had defeated the odds in one magnificent way or the other. But I wasn't inspired by those stories or by the *Reader's Digest* article at first; instead, I was privately horrified that anyone would dare compare me to a mountain climber. What people assumed would be motivational stories only served to mount the pressure of who I was apparently supposed to become. Another of Mom's friends knew an amputee, a college girl, who offered to talk to me about her experiences living on one leg. She came over a few weeks after I returned home from the hospital. When she walked into the room, a slight hitch in her gait, I wrote her off immediately: she was gorgeous, blonde, and thin. When she told me she had been a cheer-leader in high school, my jaw dropped. How did she jump around for her routines? This was who they wanted me to model myself after? There was no way I could follow in her footsteps. Where was the demented crazy person who has torn all her hair out in anger and frustration? Now *that* would be someone I could emulate. No one expected anything special from me when I had two legs, but now that I had lost one, I had to be the Disabled Role Model of the Universe? Before the accident, I didn't like running on two legs, and now I was supposed to be superhuman on one? Was this fair? I didn't appreciate those stories, because I didn't want to play the part of an inspirational amputee. But I could tell people didn't want me to go back to just being me—minus a leg. Everyone saw this as an opportunity for me to finally be something special.

And as much as I balked—as terrified as all this pressure made me feel—some small voice inside me was buying in. My situation *did* make me special. And what adolescent girl doesn't want to be extraordinary?

The morning of my first day back at school, I was sick to my stomach with fear. I had been away for four weeks, and I didn't know what to expect. Everyone I knew from school had been supportive. I'd received cards from so many people at school: the entire drama department, the cheerleading squad, and even the football team. Even so, I wasn't assured that people wouldn't treat me like a freak when I walked around school on crutches with a metal pylon—my temporary leg. When I went back to school in eighth grade after Dad died, I felt like people avoided me like the plague. If people reacted that strongly to death, how would they react to dismemberment?

Mom drove me the three miles to school. My first greeting was on the school's big reader board: "Welcome Back, Colleen." In a school of 1,800 students, it was unusual to see anyone's name on the reader board, let alone just one student's. "Oh look, Colleen, look at the sign! Isn't that so sweet?" Mom was absurdly cheerful in her typical manner. The sign did make me feel special, and my stomach settled down a bit, but I also wondered if most of the students at the school were wondering who the hell Colleen was, just like in *The Wizard of Oz*, when the witch inscribes in the sky SURRENDER DOROTHY and the munchkins all wonder, "Who's Dorothy?" I shared a kinship with Dorothy, lost in a new land with only the most basic of instructions on where to go or what to do.

I clumsily got out of the car and walked into the foyer of the school. I felt like a celebrity immediately. "Hey, Colleen, welcome back!" "Way to go, Colleen!" These words were offered by staff, friends, and strangers. A gush of warmth filled my chest, and I couldn't help but smile. Other people, the ones I was afraid of, the ones I tried to ignore, stared at me, pointed indiscreetly, and whispered out of the sides of their mouths to their friends. I could tell that suddenly everyone knew who I was, not because of my theatrical experiences, not because I had coordinated homecoming-week activities or because I was on the yearbook committee, but because I was the girl who had lost her leg in an accident. I had morphed into the school sensation. The secret part of me that felt I deserved this kind of attention, loved it. For once, there was a reason for people to remember who I was. I wasn't just a wallflower. I was special.

The one place I wouldn't be treated as special was in the presence of Beth Lewis, our drama teacher. Play rehearsal began directly after school and ran until five. Miss Lewis always sat in the back of the auditorium. She was a tall, thin woman with big lips and jowls. She wore the stylish oversized brown glasses of the late '70s, and with those on and her short, wavy, brown hair, she looked like a bug. Miss Lewis wasn't a warm, fuzzy woman. She was practical and methodical, and she took her job as director of two plays a year quite seriously. All of us high school actors joked, "You don't mess with Beth." She sat at a table littered with pastel-colored papers bearing the name of each character, her glasses dropped to the end of her nose so she could simultaneously watch us on stage and quickly jot praises or admonishments about our performance. At the end of practice, cast and crew would gather around her as she either scolded us on a bad rehearsal or praised us for a good one. When practice ended, she yelled out our character's name and, with a flick of her wrist, tossed us our feedback sheet.

Half the fun of rehearsals was hanging out backstage among the other cast members and stage crew, waiting for a cue. There were plenty of real "characters" involved in drama; I wasn't one of them. I was the giggly girl who was entertained by them and stroked their egos by laughing at their antics. Our whispered tones increased in volume over the course of every two-hour practice, interrupted only by scene changes and Miss Lewis barking orders from the cafeteria floor: "Quiet! Down!" During my first rehearsals for *Funny Girl*, everyone was very nice to me, but something had changed. I didn't feel the same kinship with these people anymore. I wanted to blame them, but I wasn't sure what to blame them for. I felt removed from the conversations and the jokes, like my four-week absence had distanced me from the intimacy a play usually inspires.

Onstage, I felt awkward. My crutches were cumbersome and hard to maneuver around the set. Following the script was difficult, words weren't coming out the way they used to, and I often forgot my lines. From the sides of their mouths, my cast mates cued me by whispering the first few words of my next line. I had played various speaking parts in previous plays, and memorizing my lines had always been easy. Now, when I read the *Funny Girl* script at home, I had a hard time concentrating on the words.

About three weeks after I'd been back at rehearsal, I received a shocking feedback sheet. "Strakosh, learn your lines," Miss Lewis had scribbled with a hard hand and lots of underlining. "Time has come when you <u>must</u> know them <u>well</u>. I'm seeing <u>absolutely</u> <u>no</u> character development growth—or growth in concentration. You just <u>must</u> learn your lines and begin to <u>focus</u> in on what is and/or should be happening on stage. You are pulling down your scenes."

My body reacted immediately and without my consent. I looked at the page to read the remarks again, but my tears made the words too blurry. The sounds in the background—the jostling of backpacks, the gossiping of my cast mates, the shuffling of feedback sheets and scripts—were sucked from the room as if by a vacuum. A fuzzy fog enveloped me.

I had been raised to respect my elders, to not question authority, to do as I was told, and to follow the rules. It wasn't in my makeup to throw that piece of paper back in her face and tell her, "Back off. I'll memorize my lines when I'm good and ready." Instead, the words pierced my brain like jolts of electricity, and I didn't have the bandwidth to assimilate them gracefully.

Internally—but only internally—I gave way to an explosion of protest. *I have to focus on what's happening on stage? I can hardly focus on what's happening in my life. I don't know where I am or where I belong.*

Memorize my lines? How about memorizing a new way to walk? How about memorizing the twelve-inch scar on the leg that was saved? How about memorizing the image of the man who ripped a part of my body away from me?

I'm pulling down my scenes? She doesn't know what it's like to have a pulled-down scene. Just seven weeks ago, I had one hell of a pulled-down scene.

No character growth? Aren't I doing enough?

I looked up at her, begging the tears in my eyes to evaporate before she saw them, but they didn't, and she did. Her eyes widened, and she took a step back as she noticed the intensity of my reaction. "Opening night is three and a half weeks away, Colleen." Her eyes held a desperate plea. *Please be okay. We all need you to be okay.*

I knew what I had to do. I didn't want to put the rest of the cast at risk because I wasn't memorizing my lines. These people had all been so generous, kind, and supportive since the accident. The least I could do was memorize my lines. This play was what mattered most right then.

I decided to do what I was told even though this play was a bigger commitment than I really wanted. What I really wanted was to cry and scream, to throw things, to be alone with Harvey, the man who hit me, in a small room for a whole day so I could rip him apart, limb by limb. But good Catholic girls didn't act vicious, let alone think evil thoughts of violence. Good Catholic girls did what they were told. And so I gulped down my hostility and got ready for my performance.

Opening night of any play was always a big deal. The stage crew often decorated the casts' hallway lockers, sentimental notes were shared among the cast and crew in the dressing room, Miss Lewis always wrote an encouraging note to each member of the cast and crew, and my family always had flowers for me and signs reading BREAK A LEG! But opening night of *Funny Girl* was something special. As well as getting all the normal opening-night kudos, I received so much more. Rob was there to sit beside my family and cheer me on. My physical therapist sent me a dozen roses, my aunts and uncles came to my performance, and even Miss Lewis sent me flowers. Though Sandy, the girl playing Fanny Brice with full comedic force and a lyrical voice, was the leading lady, I felt like the star of the show opening night. While I loved all the attention, something kept nagging at me. Something elusive, irksome, and true. Why am I receiving such praise now? And what am I really receiving praise for? Why are people so proud of me? And what does their pride really mean in terms of what is expected of me?

I made it through our performances the best I could. Each night we received a standing ovation, and I smiled and waved at the audience with the rest of the cast. But after our final performance, when we were finally striking the set, I realized that I couldn't strike this new role from my life, not entirely. I wasn't Mrs. Strakosh anymore, but I had set a precedent for being the brave survivor.

Two weeks before graduation, I was sitting at the kitchen table trying to study for a final exam, and I was having a hard time focusing.

The front door opened, and Mom escorted the parish priest and two of my high school teachers, Mr. Sanders and Miss Lewis, into the room. I was stunned and confused. Though Father Dave visited often, having teachers in the house was a rarity. They all sat down around the table and handed me a letter.

I glanced around at all their expectant faces, wondering what was going on, and when Mom nodded that I should open the envelope, I obeyed and took out the hand-written note inside. As I read it, I realized what was happening. Mr. Sanders had talked about this last fall, but I had completely forgotten about it. He had planned a summer trip to Asia for students, to be led by him and his wife. What I slowly started to put together was that people from school, church, and the hospital had all donated money to enable me to go on this thousand-dollar trip. I tried to hide the panic. I tried to mask my fear. As I was learning to do, I revealed only excitement and joy. I could see the pride and happiness on all their faces. They were so pleased they had kept this a secret from me over the past two months. Through shared laughter, they all told stories of how I had walked in on conversations they were having about the trip and how they had each almost ruined the surprise.

But under my smiling face, I was wondering, *How will I do this? Won't this require a lot of walking?* I had never left home for a month before or traveled outside the United States. *No one asked me if I wanted to go!* The good girl in me felt guilty for even thinking such ungracious thoughts. The trip was so huge and unknown, though. My life already felt so huge and unknown. I was barraged with kindness and good intentions, and I felt the mounting pressure to perform once again. The play was over, but now I felt like I was playing a part in a life-play. This part had been thrown into my lap—the role of a lifetime.

I knew I didn't want this part. I hadn't auditioned for this part; I hadn't rehearsed. This part had no script—in fact, the script was being written day by day, moment by moment. I didn't have control over where the script was going. And people around me had creative license to add whatever scenes they pleased, like a four-week trip to Asia. Being the star of this play, I had to ad-lib my way through each scene. My family, friends, teachers, and doctors were like audience members, observing my every move, smiling, clapping, laughing, crying, watching me play my new part—so invested that I didn't feel I could let them down. And so I knew I would perform, whether I wanted to or not.

One of these new parts was playing the Golden Girl of the senior class. Because I survived the accident and resumed normal life so quickly, I received multiple end-of-the-year awards: the Girl of the Year award from the Signet Society; one of the top ten seniors of the year as chosen by the senior class; the distinction of being in the National Registry of top seniors; and three college scholarships. The accolades kept coming, and the praises boosted me up, all with the veneer of a promise that I was something special. But deep down, a hollowness whispered to me when I was alone and told me I wouldn't have received any of these awards or scholarships if I hadn't lost my leg. I dared not admit it to anyone for fear of being ungrateful, but I knew if I were truly standing on my own *two* feet, this wouldn't all be happening. I wouldn't even have my deepening relationship with Rob. I was just beginning to figure out that who I was on the inside didn't matter—only who I was on the outside. I had to lose a part of myself to be something special.

6

• ● •

SEEKING COMFORT

In *Star Trek: The Next Generation*, a species called the Borg is united by a collective consciousness. Each humanoid is identified by their place in the collective: "seven of nine," say, or "two of ten." Growing up in my family, as the fourth child, I was "six of eight." We were the proverbial "all for one and one for all" family. There was great comfort in growing up absorbed in this collective. We laughed alike, prayed alike, thought alike, and eventually we would be expected to vote alike.

Catholicism was infused into our clan. Our faith defined us as a unit and was integral to our family's identity. Our social circle was centered around the church and our Catholic grade school. Mom and Dad's faith guided their decisions about how we served our community and helped others. We were so close, it was like we were different aspects of one being.

Mom and Dad had six children in eight years. Although we were tightly knit, each of my siblings had a distinct quality that distinguished them as a unique thread. The eldest, Maureen, had a sharp mind; Mary Beth, who came next, was the musically talented one; Kevin, the eldest boy, was Dad's constant companion on fishing and hunting trips. I was convinced he was Dad's favorite. Then there was me—every family has one—nondescript, vague, nothing special. This is how I had always seen myself and how I assumed everyone else saw me, too. Matthew and David, the two youngest boys, were like two peas in a pod: they were loud, funny, obnoxious, and endearing. I desperately looked to my siblings to see who I was, but the reflection was vague. I saw I was a Haggerty, I was Democrat, and I was supposed to be funny and kind; but I could never see the specifics of who I was.

I was thirteen years old when Dad died. All six of us children banded around my mother in support like white blood cells enveloping an infection, for she appeared to be the one most deeply affected. Her pain was our pain. We selflessly gave up social events to stay home and keep her company. We ensured her birthday, their wedding anniversary, and all major holidays were as happy as possible. We made homemade gifts oozing with meaning and sentimentality. And during those first grief-filled years, we each learned empathy skills and became highly sensitive to others' pain. While on the outside it looked as though our collective had dwindled, we held to Dad's spirit and memory so tightly that he retained a place in the whole.

But in the midst of that loss, I still felt as dull as the winter skies of my native Washington. I'd wanted to stand out, to peek through the clouds and sparkle some of my uniqueness to my family and to the world, but I figured that wasn't my fate. God's plan for me was to be plain. I knew my place; I knew what part I played in our collective. I was the shy one. I was the baby girl. I was the wallflower. No one seemed to expect much from me other than to show up and be kind.

In those earlier years before high school, I only had one friend, Patty. I would look at her when we were together and try to see who I was in her eyes, but again, the vision was cloudy. What Patty reflected was my sweetness, my quietness, and my occasional daring spirit. She and I got along so well I never had a chance to understand how to be in a relationship with another person while exposing and accepting the differences between two people.

Because of the closeness of my family and my relationship with Patty, I reached adolescence confused about where I ended and other people began. After my accident, I couldn't have been more different from other people—or more separate from them. My amputation catapulted me into a distant universe, and yet here I was, still living on Earth. The only evidence I had that I was still here was my body—my now-deformed and ugly body. Though my family was a great source of comfort to me, they were also my most frequent reminder that I was now alienated, cut out from their normality. When we were young, Mom and Dad demonstrated the waltz and the Lindy to us, and we would sometimes spontaneously get up from the dinner table and dance. After my accident, when the urge to dance first hit my family, I froze. *How do I do this? How do I even try without looking like a moron?* If there was a safe place to put on my gimpy dancing shoes, it should have been with my family. If there were people who could make me feel proud of myself for trying, it would have been my clan. And if there were men who could get me to twirl with glee under their strong, capable arms, they were my brothers. But I knew I was no longer like them.

I experienced the way people looked at me in the real world. The looks of admiration and pity. The look that, even though I couldn't name it yet, said, "Wow, you're so brave. I admire you, but I wouldn't want to be you." I could tolerate that from outsiders, but I couldn't risk seeing those pitying looks on the faces of my family members.

The longer I lived as an amputee and the more being one-legged became my new normal, the more the compliments bothered me because they marked me as insufficient. These comments told me that people saw something to be compensated for in the fact that I was an amputee. More to the point, the praises of strangers let me know that I was being seen not for who I was, but for what I was missing.

No one in my world knew my internal experience, my secret world, my spirit world, the tender, quiet, child part of me that was impacted by my amputation. And their questions and accolades couldn't and didn't touch this part. This sacred, hidden part was difficult to articulate, name, or even understand. Every day I was drowning in a deeper chasm of insecurity and doubt, and I was desperate for some form of relief.

That summer I told Rob, "I want to start smoking." I was surprised to hear the words come out of my mouth, but once they did, they rang true. I needed something to help me calm down.

"Well then, go ahead," he said. I was taken aback. Rob had strong opinions about a lot of things, and he made it clear he didn't like cigarettes. Rob was my world, and his go-ahead was all I needed.

Turning to cigarettes was the only way I knew how to deal with the feelings I was stuffing into the depths of my heart. By the time I confessed to Rob that I wanted to start smoking, I was on the verge of bursting. My feelings were a jumbled mess of sadness, anger, resentment, rage, and fear. Adapting to my prosthetic leg slowed down the physical pace in my life, but everything else was swirling past me at warp speed. Losing my leg tore my world apart, and I felt like my life had been put back together with clapboard; there was no solid foundation to me anymore.

When I sat alone with a cigarette, I could slow down and think. As the smoke swirled around me, I was enveloped in my own little world. I escaped, if only for a few minutes, the unspoken expectations from everyone else that I be happy and positive. It was my time to numb out.

7

. ● .

BODY OR SOUL?

I ended up attending my first-choice university, which was two hours from my home. I spent most of the first semester racking up phone bills talking to Rob. We were miserable without each other, so he enrolled and moved up for second semester.

In April of 1980, during my second year of college, I finally had my day in court with Harvey, the man who hit me with his green Pacer and took my leg from me—and so much more. For the rest of my life I would retain only about two hours of fragmented memories of that weeklong trial. I was told I couldn't communicate with Harvey because we were adversaries. I sat at the prosecutor's table between my mom and my lawyer, sneaking peaks at Harvey, who sat at the defendant's table with his head cast down. My lawyer told me that he had ulcers. I was happy that he was suffering in some way, but I also felt guilty for my happiness. When I took the witness stand, my lawyer lauded me for having never been to therapy. He praised my strength and determination in the face of adversity. This only reinforced that I was doing the right thing by stuffing my feelings. There was a moment when I looked at nearly all the adults in my world from up on that stand and wished they would teach me how to deal with my feelings, instead of teaching me how to stuff them.

In the end, the jury was divided in their understanding of exactly where the accident had happened. My lawyer could tell they were going to be a hung jury, which meant we'd have to go through the whole, painful process again. We ended up settling and I received a tenth of the amount we asked for. Early on in the process of preparing for the trial, my lawyer explained that this trial was really my insurance company suing Harvey's insurance company, so when we settled, I felt betrayed by Harvey himself. He should have stood up in court and demanded that I be fairly compensated. I had a lifetime of prosthetic legs to buy, years of physical therapy, massage therapy, and acupuncture—as well as doctor appointments—to pay for in my future.

After the trial was over, one juror came up to me and explained that one female juror—ironically, the one my lawyer thought would be most sensitive to my case—thought the accident was my fault. Her opinion had hung the jury.

The moment I heard that she blamed me, though I was physically incapable of running, my body mercifully carried me quickly through the courtroom, down the hall, and into the stairwell. Mary Beth was right behind me, and when we closed the stairwell door, we both screamed and wept in each other's arms. How could that juror say the accident was my fault? Didn't I do the right thing by getting out of the car on that snowy day to flag down help? Harvey was the idiot who was driving too fast. Mary Beth kept apologizing, saying she should have made me stay in the car, but she wasn't the one who I needed to hear from. The trial was over, and Harvey had left the courtroom without talking to me.

Mary Beth and I stayed in the stairwell until we were able to catch our breath. I wiped my nose with the sleeve of my shirt and looked at my sister's face, which was blotchy and red like mine. Holding her gaze, I knew that the accident was not our fault. Not mine, not hers. But we were united in this suspended guilt/grief state. That green Pacer had changed both of our lives forever. Though we would handle our feelings differently, and the consequences of the accident would be different for each of us, we would be on the same journey in search of healing and freedom from the burden we carried together.

I went back to school when the trial was over and resumed life as though I had not just faced the man whose car had cut off my leg. In early June, I began mysteriously waking up to intense nausea. It sat in my stomach like a bad meal refusing to digest. I grew so frustrated that I resorted to sticking my toothbrush down my throat to get the sickening feeling out of me. I didn't understand what was happening, and I was embarrassed that my roommate Laurie could hear me throwing up from her bedroom next door to the bathroom. But curiously, I only felt sick in the morning. Maybe I should have guessed what was going on, but after I made myself throw up, I usually felt fine and went about my day like it had never happened.

This was my first experience living away from home outside of the dorms, and I wasn't sure what I should do about my ongoing sickness. Within a few weeks, the nausea was getting worse and lasting throughout the day. I knew pot was good for nausea, so on a Wednesday afternoon after classes, I asked Laurie for a joint. We lived in a house on top of a well-populated hill overlooking a bay. After classes, we often sat in the two overstuffed chairs facing the picture window to talk about our respective days. That Wednesday, we assumed our usual positions in the rockers overlooking the bay and lit up.

"Colleen, do you think you might be pregnant?" She took a hit and passed the joint to me. A completely different nausea filled me—the queasiness of fear.

"Pregnant?" I blurted out, coughing and sputtering on the smoke I'd just inhaled. "I can't be pregnant. No way!" For most people, the suggestion of pregnancy as an explanation for my symptoms would have made immediate sense. But for me, the girl who had spent the last two years ignoring her deeper feelings just to get through each day, ignoring hard truths was right in my wheelhouse.

"So what birth control do you use?" she asked, looking me right in the eyes.

"The rhythm method. We're just really careful. I heard Mom and

Dad used the rhythm method." I looked down at the joint, not really seeing it.

"Yeah, and how many kids did *they* have?" she said, laughing. I swallowed the lump in my throat as I thought of the six of us, results of the rhythm method. I felt my face flush and my stomach sink to the floor as I realized I could actually be pregnant. I handed the joint back to Laurie before taking another hit.

Everything in me contracted. *NO! NO! NO! NO! NO!*

"Oh my God. I have to call Rob." I got up out of my chair and went to the phone and dialed, desperately pleading inside for him to answer. He picked up after the third ring, and I begged him to come over right away. "I'll explain when you get here."

I went back to the living room to sit with Laurie. "Colleen, I think you should call Planned Parenthood and make an appointment for a pregnancy test," Laurie said. She took another hit and then snuffed out the joint. This was all happening so fast, but I knew she was right. Laurie got up, found the phone book, and dialed the number. I made an appointment and then waited, sitting in the chair and looking out to the water and the seagulls, a rising terror growing in my heart about what my future would hold now.

Rob arrived about a half hour later. I ran up to him, panicky and trembling. It didn't help that I was mildly stoned. I grabbed his arms and looked up into his face. "I might be . . ." I could hardly say the word "pregnant." I buried my face in the crook of his neck and began to sob. He wrapped his arms around me and shushed and comforted me with his gentle voice, while inwardly I reproached myself.

How could I have let this happen? I'm so stupid.
What will Mom say? Oh God, I can't tell Mom.
If I can't tell Mom, what do I do?
She thinks I'm a good Catholic girl.

Rob led me up to my room, and we lay on the bed, with me curled against his chest. I cried, fretted, and worried. I had no idea what to do. "Colleen, baby, everything will be okay. Let's just wait and see what they say at your appointment tomorrow. Who knows, maybe you just have the flu," he reassured me.

The next day, Rob and I had to skip our morning classes to make my ten a.m. appointment. Planned Parenthood was downtown, about four miles away, so Rob insisted we take a taxi; we didn't know the buses well, and he knew I couldn't comfortably walk that far. I appreciated the extravagance.

I was asked to give a urine sample. As I sat on the toilet, I was trembling so much that I peed more on my hand than into the cup. Saying a silent prayer—something I'd vowed not to do when I was in the hospital—I held the cup in my hand. It was still warm from my pee. *Please don't let me be pregnant. Please.* I went to the exam room, sat in the chair, and wrung my clammy hands. *Please don't let me be pregnant. Please . . .*

As usual, God failed me. A tall, stocky, middle-aged nurse bustled into the room with my test results, all business. "Well, it looks like you're pregnant. What do you want to do?" I sat on my hands to avoid wringing them any further and looked at the floor in shame. What was I going to *do*? I had no idea. There was no precedent for this in my world. I didn't know anyone who'd gotten pregnant outside of marriage. *I'm such a bad person. I'm worse than bad*, I ruminated.

"Can I get my boyfriend?"

She looked at her watch and sighed. "Yeah, sure."

I walked out to the lobby, my legs hardly holding me up. I saw Rob's face immediately and beckoned him to me. He rose quickly and scurried over.

"I'm pregnant," I whispered, catching him up before we walked into the room. Rob nodded, grabbed my hand, and gave it a supportive squeeze. I sat down in the one available chair, and Rob stood beside me, holding on to my shoulder. We waited for the nurse to stop writing down her notes. After what felt like an eternity, she looked up at us over the top of her glasses.

"So, do you two have a plan for this pregnancy?"

Rob and I looked at each other. "No, we don't," Rob answered softly.

"Well, you basically have three choices. You can proceed with the pregnancy and have the baby, you can give the baby up for adoption, or you can terminate the pregnancy."

I looked at her hands and noticed she was wearing a wedding ring. *Does she have children?* I wondered. *She must think I'm awful, getting pregnant without being married. She must think I'm the scum of the earth.*

Rob and I couldn't respond. I just sat there. The swirls in the tile floor swam in front of me as tears welled in my eyes. I couldn't believe this was happening. What would Mom do? What would people think of me? How could I possibly handle this? I'd hardly adjusted to a new vision of my life as an amputee. I could barely see what my future would look like as I made my way through it with only one leg. Even if I closed my eyes tightly and concentrated hard—which I did while the nurse and Rob stood by waiting—I couldn't summon in this moment my childhood vision of my life as a mother.

The nurse's voice softened and so did her eyes. "You have some time to think about this. Here's the number of an ob-gyn who can help you with whatever decision you make." Then she narrowed her focus on me, and her voice carried the admonishing tone of a Catholic nun. "And I strongly suggest you also talk to the doctor about birth control."

"How much does an abortion cost?" Rob asked the nurse. I jerked my head up and looked at him, stunned. My face flushed in embarrassment. How could he ask such a bold and loaded question so casually?

"About three hundred dollars," the nurse answered matter-of-factly.

What was this? A business deal? Didn't my feelings or opinions matter? My breathing became shallow. I felt a pit in my stomach and dread in my heart.

"Well, thank you very much," Rob said, taking the piece of paper from the nurse.

We all stood up, and I grabbed Rob's hand. We paid for the office visit, and Rob called for a taxi to take us back to my house. As we waited outside, I was too afraid to say anything. Rob was quiet, too, which unnerved me further. He started rubbing my back softly, like we were in this together, but it sounded like he'd already made his decision. I wanted him to leave me alone, so I walked around the corner of the building, not wanting him to notice my tears, which were flowing heavily.

Goddamn it! Hadn't my body betrayed me enough? Hadn't I been through enough? How could God let this happen to me? After the accident, everyone told me God doesn't give us more than we can handle. Well, I couldn't handle this! This was way too much for me. I couldn't be pregnant. I couldn't carry a child for nine months. I hardly knew how to get through each day. People thought I was handling my amputation well, but I wasn't. They had no idea.

After walking tentatively around the corner, Rob said, "Colleen, we can't have this baby." His voice was soft and low.

"Goddamn it, I know!" I yelled, taking a few steps away from him. How could he be so quick to want to throw this away, while I still couldn't believe it was even true? I didn't want to deal with this at all. My love for Rob was so deep it was like breathing to me. We'd been together two years; I wanted nothing more than to marry him, plan a family, do all this the *right* way, but by now I also knew Rob wasn't cut out for it. I trusted Rob's deep love for me, but he was a free spirit. He had places to go, literally, and he was a solo traveler. Though I had a huge place in his heart, he could live without me. I wasn't sure I could live without him. He'd helped me redefine myself after I lost my leg, and I believed if I lost him, I'd be losing another part of myself. But I knew, too, he wanted this baby to go away so he wouldn't be *forced* to stay with me. He needed to know he could leave whenever he wanted and not be tied down to a family. I looked at him now and saw how much he'd given me. I could feel the familiar need to protect others from my suffering. I couldn't indulge the anger I felt. Instead, I needed to consider what to do. The choice would not be easy; the risk of loss would be great no matter what I did. What was I most willing to lose—Rob or myself? And wouldn't I lose a piece of myself no matter what I decided?

The taxi arrived, and we both got in, distant and silent. I stared out the window as we drove home, wishing it would rain. Hard. I couldn't appreciate the flowers or the sun glistening off the water in the bay. I wanted to crawl into bed, listen to the steady beat of the rain on the roof, and hear it echo the pounding of my heart.

After my accident, I had been exalted as a survivor. Peers and adults looked to me as a shining example of how beautifully one can rise above a tragic turn of events. What I considered basic survival everyone else viewed as admirable. What would they think of me now? I knew I couldn't take a chance on a baby right now, not when I was still figuring out my life—not only as a college student, but also as an amputee. The pregnancy alone could do me in. I'd been warned that if I gained weight, my prosthetic leg wouldn't fit me any longer. How would I walk if that happened? How could I even bend over and put it on to begin with? But on the other hand, how could I have an abortion? As far from God as I felt, a huge part of me was as Catholic as I'd ever been.

The particular timing of the pregnancy was terrible for other reasons besides the fact that I wasn't ready to become a mother. I was scheduled to return home that weekend to attend my brother Matthew's high school graduation. I had already made arrangements to take the Greyhound bus to Seattle, and while I was dreading the thought of a stuffy two-hour bus ride, I dreaded even more seeing my family.

Would anyone be able to tell I was pregnant? Would my mom take one look at me and simply *know*? There was no getting around it. Family obligation dictated I show up, even if I said I felt ill.

Friday came, and I woke up feeling sicker than ever. I had to throw up repeatedly. Each time I slid my toothbrush down my throat, I wished the tiny germ of a fetus would come up with my vomit. Each wave gripped my stomach, and the skin on my torso tingled uncomfortably, like it would if I were hearing fingers on a chalkboard. A ring of cold sweat glistened around the perimeter of my face. I wanted to heave this interloper out of me. I couldn't stop crying. I skipped classes again that day because I couldn't muster the energy to walk the half mile to campus. I lay in bed, exhausted in a way I had never experienced, not even in the hospital. I drifted in and out of a light sleep, skimming over dreams that felt so real. I saw myself with long greasy hair and bloodshot eyes surrounded by dark circles, sitting alone on the altar at church, the whole congregation pointing at me, scowling, condemning me to hell. I saw myself weighing over three hundred pounds, full of fat and baby, stuck in the overstuffed chair in the living room, unable to get up, unable to walk because my leg didn't fit me anymore.

I awoke to my own sobbing.

When Rob came over to take me to the bus station, I was still in bed. He kissed me softly on my eyelids. "Colleen, we have to leave in half an hour or you'll miss the bus. You haven't even showered?" I heard the care and concern in his voice. "Here, let me help you get up." I wanted to resist, but Rob pulled the blankets from me and gently pulled me out of bed. I knew I had to put this crying jag on hold and hurry, but every movement felt heavy, like trying to swim through quicksand. As I showered, fighting the incoming tide of my emotions, which threatened to flood over me, Rob haphazardly packed my things.

I didn't want to leave Rob, but I couldn't think of any way to get out of this. In my family, we were always there for one another—no matter what. After a tearful good-bye, I picked up my bag, which was infinitely lighter than my heart, and boarded the bus.

I was late getting to the bus station, and the only seats available were in the back row, near the gas fumes. I stored my bag and sat down near a window. As the bus lurched forward, so did my stomach. I swallowed the bile and lay my head against the cold, sweaty window, wondering if I should tell Mom and simply face her admonishments. Just the thought made my stomach heave again. What would she say? I could imagine her screaming. I could see her yelling at me. But mostly, I could see the disappointment in her eyes. It would be bad enough to admit to Mom I was having sex. Aside from the moment in my hospital room, right after the accident, she and I never talked about it; I just assumed she knew Rob and I made love, but I didn't know for sure. Good Catholic girls don't have sex before marriage. She certainly didn't. But to tell her about a pregnancy, too? I thought about how people must feel in those rags-to-riches stories—how they go from being a nobody to a somebody—like the actress Jean Harlow, who was "discovered" at a drugstore hamburger counter and skyrocketed to stardom. I knew a little of what sudden fame felt like. I knew what it was like to have people's view of you change. After my accident, I went from being the quiet wallflower of the family to the admirable survivor. I didn't want to fall from grace. People would scorn me. They would be so deeply disappointed in me. No one would understand that I secretly lived a numb existence and that being with Rob was the only thing that even touched on a sense of vitality or reality for me.

On the ride into Seattle, gas fumes and fear rolled into a toxic ball in my stomach. The bus pulled into the station, and I could see Mom waiting outside and my youngest brother, David, standing beside her. I dreaded the thought of meeting Mom's eyes, certain she would be able to tell I was pregnant just by looking at me. I grabbed my bag from the overhead compartment and walked down the aisle, willing myself forward. I took the three steps off the bus one by one, as I do with all steps because of my prosthetic leg. I looked up and saw Mom waiting near the foot of the stairs, grinning widely. But when she took a closer look at me, she gasped. "Colleen, you look horrible!" she clucked, her motherly concern kicking in. "Are you okay?" She pulled me into her and hugged me tightly. I knew I didn't deserve her compassion.

"Oh, I just feel sick. I had to sit at the back of the bus, and the fumes got to me." I hugged her back, wishing she could take this all away from me, wishing I could be a little girl again, sitting on her lap. I stifled the tears; she wouldn't understand them.

"Oh, honey, I'm sorry. You'll feel better once we get home."

I gave David a quick hug, and we headed for the car.

On the half-hour drive home, Mom asked about school. I talked about everything I could think of just to keep the conversation going. I rolled down the window, once again feeling sick.

When we got home, I went to my bedroom to lie down. My room, our house, held so many wonderful memories of growing up. Could I possibly ever recreate this kind of safety and joy for a child? With stark and sudden clarity, I understood that my childhood dream had been thrown out the window when I lost my leg—and that's why I couldn't imagine it anymore, no matter how hard I tried. Even if I had six kids, I wouldn't be like my mom. I would be an amputee mom.

I dozed in and out of a light sleep, unable to keep the nausea at bay. I finally went into the bathroom and tried my toothbrush trick to vomit, but I only gagged loudly. I swallowed and swallowed until there was nothing left to swallow. I tried to be quiet, but the bathroom was next to Mom's bedroom, and she heard me. I heard her feet scamper to the bathroom doorway. She knocked lightly and spoke to me from the other side of the door.

"Colleen, this doesn't sound like car sickness. Should I be worried?" She sounded genuinely concerned.

"No, I just don't feel good, Mom. I'll go lie back down."

"Well, we're supposed to leave in half an hour," she reminded me. "You should really be getting ready."

In a panic, I got up off the bathroom floor, wiped my face, and opened the door. Mom's eyes held a mixture of worry and impatience.

"Do you think you can even go?" she asked.

"I don't know!" I yelled, not intending to. Of course I didn't think I could go. But I would.

She looked as shocked at my outburst as I was. "Don't take that tone with me, Colleen. I'm sorry if you're not feeling well, but this is Matthew's graduation." I was the good girl, not one to yell at my mother. She and I got along well; that was the expectation. The one thing I wanted was to have her help me, but even for as loving as she was, I didn't believe she could handle this.

"I'm sorry, Mom," I said, hating that I was whining, and feeling bad for snapping at her, for doing anything to erode our relationship. "I'll hurry and get ready." I put on my nice pants and a shirt and went back to the bathroom to freshen up. Brushing my teeth and putting on makeup helped me feel a little better. I kept swallowing the bile. I kept swallowing my fear and my urge to fall apart.

My five siblings were downstairs waiting. I hadn't seen them for about a month. I gave hugs all around, stifling the sadness that crept up.

"What's the matter, Coll?" asked Mary Beth.

"I got really carsick on the bus ride down."

Mom cut in, hustling us out the door. "Kids, we need to get to the auditorium. Everyone in the car!"

At the high school, about a half hour into the graduation program, a wave of nausea swept through me, threatening to explode. I had to get to a bathroom NOW. I stood up. "Excuse me, I have to get to the bathroom." People scurried out of my way. Navigating through the myriad of legs with my clunky prosthetic was tricky. I was slowed down further when I got to the aisle and had to descend the stairs one at a time because of my leg. My stomach lurched. I kept swallowing, cursing my leg for slowing me down. I hurried to the bathroom, got into a stall, locked the door, and threw up into the toilet. Sweat beaded on my forehead, and anger and frustration covered me like a fog.

I knelt on the floor with my head over the bowl and flashed back to my own graduation—how I'd been both on the top of the world, reveling in the admiration of everyone who saw me as a victor in the face of adversity, and battling daily fantasies of ripping the head off of the man who had taken away my leg. Those were confusing days, but not as confusing as this one.

I unrolled some toilet paper and wiped my brow and then my mouth. Then I heard someone come in. "Colleen, are you okay?" It was Maureen.

"I'm better now. I guess this is more than just car sickness."

"I guess so. Mom's worried about you. Can you make it through the ceremony?"

"Yeah, I'll be fine. But I should sit in an aisle seat, just in case."

We walked back to our row, and everyone moved down a seat so I could sit on the aisle. I spent the next two hours wiping my sweaty brow and praying to God to take the nausea away. I just needed to get through the ceremony without any more vomit. I did.

Afterward, we headed home, leaving Matthew to go to a party with his friends.

As soon as we got to the house, I went straight to my room and fell into bed. Sleep came quickly. I woke the next morning to another wave of nausea. I was getting tired of this. I lay in bed, hoping to keep it at bay by just lying still. About an hour later, Mom came into my room. She sat down on the bed and felt my forehead.

"No fever. Colleen, I'm really concerned." Did her face have a hint of anger, or was I just imagining it? "Could you could be pregnant?" Her eyes were hard and her tone accusatory.

"No, Mom!" I squeaked. "I guess I just have the stomach flu." I don't know how I got those words out. I wasn't used to lying to my mother, but there it was; I had just done it. Lying to my mother was about the biggest thing in the world. Just strike me down dead right now.

"Well, you just rest awhile, and we'll see how you're doing later." She got up and left, leaving me heartsick as well.

I spent the day in bed knowing I had to act sick all day to feign having the flu. I knew I'd give myself away if I got up and acted fine.

I spent the day trying to study for my finals, but I was distracted by the decision I had to make. I longed to tell Mom, but I couldn't imagine saying the words to her. When she was my age, she was pregnant with her second child. Her life had always been my dream, but I knew now I would never have it. A whisper of change blew through my heart, leaving me feeling empty.

If ever there was a supportive family, it was mine, but I couldn't imagine my family supporting me in this—what I was about to do. I would tarnish the Haggerty name. At our church, we were all seen as Goody Two-shoes. After Dad's death and my accident, the whole church rallied around us in support. It was hard to admit to myself that I had already made my decision about whether or not I'd keep the baby. Abortion went against everything I had been taught as a Catholic. It was a mortal sin. But as foreign and unthinkable as the decision felt, the path of abortion was a lot easier to imagine than having a baby. If I said yes to an abortion, it would all be over soon. If I said yes to a child, I would be walking into a lifetime of unknowns. I already felt like my life was full of unknowns: Rob, a career, my own ability to function independently, let alone as a single mother with one working leg. How would I support us? How would I finish college? How could I chase my young child away from streets and pool edges, or jump up and stop his tilting chair from toppling over? How could I exercise my greatest instincts as a mother—to protect him, at all costs? The insecurity—my sense of inadequacy—swamped me. I was terrified by the prospect of it all. I didn't even know how my leg would affect *me* for the rest of my life, let alone me as a mother. I was determined to live as normal a life as possible, but sometimes, those parameters felt impossibly narrow.

The next morning, I woke up feeling sick, as usual, but also relieved that I was going back to college—and better still, back to Rob. I was not looking forward to the bus ride, but it ended up being easier than I imagined.

When I arrived at the station, Rob was standing outside with a taxi waiting. I fell into his quick embrace, exhausted. He kissed my eyelids gently and opened the door to the taxi. On the drive home, I put my head on his shoulder and surrendered to the relief of being back in his arms and not having to hide my pregnancy from my family anymore. "How did it go?" he asked as he stroked my hair.

"It was hard." I paused, reflecting on my conversation with Mom the previous day, the guilt washing over me. "Mom asked me if I was pregnant, and . . ." I choked out the last words, "I lied to her." Rob knew how close Mom and I were, and he held me tightly.

Back at my house, we finally had a chance to talk about what to do.

We went upstairs to my room for privacy and sat on the edge of my bed. "Rob, I know you don't want this baby. I don't want it, either. But I don't know how to do this." I looked down at my belly, placed my hands on it. "Isn't this a baby?" I looked into his eyes, searching for an answer.

He cleared his throat, sat up straight, furrowed his brow, and looked me in the eye. "I don't think so. Right now, it's smaller than your thumbnail. It's just a collection of cells." He shifted on the bed to face me directly. "Who knows when it's a baby, but I know it's not one now," he said with authority.

We stared at each other for a moment, me wanting to believe him, him wanting to convince me. He did.

We made an appointment to have the procedure done later in the week. We both had finals to study for, but we couldn't concentrate. The days dragged by, filled with nausea and dread. I felt clammy and lightheaded. Since I had made the decision, I just wanted it over with.

On the day of our appointment, I walked into the doctor's office knowing this experience would change me forever. I was giving up a huge part of who I was so I could become who I knew I needed to be. So why did I feel so sad and guilty? Would the soul I carried inside me forgive me? Somehow I knew it was a boy. Where would he go once I terminated the pregnancy? My dwindling Catholic sensibility didn't provide any answers to my questions.

I lay on the table with Rob by my head, stroking my hair as the doctor asked me to put my feet in the awkward stirrups and scoot myself down to the end of the table. He explained the procedure was like vacuuming out my uterus, and all I could imagine was a tube sucking away the tiny speck of a baby. I couldn't stop curling my five toes. I couldn't stop crying. If only it didn't actually sound like a vacuum, I might have been okay. "I'm so sorry. I'm so sorry. I'm so sorry." I don't know if I actually said the words aloud. I felt deep remorse and anguish, and all I could do was apologize to the baby that would never be, to my God who I distrusted as much as I wished I could believe in him, and to who I used to be—a virtuous Catholic girl.

There are precious, holy moments in life—not "sweet precious," but "tender and vulnerable precious"—that need holding. They don't come around very often, but this was one of those moments. In my hands, I carried a prayer with a desperate plea for forgiveness. I didn't know how this moment would change the course of my life, but I instinctively knew it would.

The vacuuming didn't take long. Afterward, the doctor talked to us about birth control and fitted me for a diaphragm. I disliked how it would always remind me of that fateful day when I said no to one life so I could keep having my own.

Back at home, Rob and I quietly and slowly walked up the stairs to my room. I wasn't nauseated anymore, but now I was sick in a different, more lasting way. I stood at the threshold of my bedroom and looked at my bed, still unmade, and my desk with my homework piled neatly, just as it had been when I left in the morning. I saw my dirty clothes in the hamper and my clean clothes hanging in the closet. None of these things had changed, yet everything looked different. I was reminded of coming home from the hospital after my accident and going to my bedroom for the first time. When I left my bedroom the morning of the accident, I had two legs. I returned two weeks later with only one. I was returning to this bedroom with something missing, too.

After the abortion, I felt like I had lost another body part. I had a gnawing feeling deep in my stomach, around the place a fetus would be, similar to the phantom pain I felt in my missing limb. Rob and I climbed into bed and curled around each other. I quietly sobbed in regret and relief while Rob held me tight.

After my accident, the shroud of my grief had morphed into a hard shell, a protective layer between me and the world. I felt like I always had an invisible suit of armor on. As I lay in Rob's arms, I felt the armor thicken, protecting me further from the world, from my feelings, from pain.

The following week, I took my finals, wondering what the hell I was doing. Everything had changed now. I knew Rob and I wouldn't get married now that we had said no to having a child together. I didn't know what to do with myself. I felt lost. My lousy grades indicated I should drop out of college and figure out where I was headed.

I went home to live with Mom the summer after the abortion. I hadn't seen her since Matthew's graduation. We never talked about the flu I had, and I was glad she didn't bring it up because I was too ashamed to lie again. But still, I was not pleasant to be around. I was depressed, but fighting it. And my hormones, which had started doing their job when I was pregnant, but were then misdirected, were reorienting themselves. I felt perpetually premenstrual and directed all my anger inward. Now that I had had the abortion, I was regretting it terribly. While I knew I couldn't have gone through with the pregnancy and still maintained my current level of mobility, I was angry with myself for compromising the values and beliefs I'd grown up with—those that I'd once held so personal and dear. From my feelings of selfishness, the deep gnawing in my stomach grew.

Rob lived with his parents that summer, and we continued to

see each other, but I could read the writing on the wall. Our relationship was dying a slow death, but neither one of us wanted it to end. In spite of what we knew we had to do, we continued to date. I needed to be near him, to stay connected to the person who had gone through such an intense and life-altering event with me, but his usually delightful sense of humor couldn't coax me into laughter or keep the depression at bay. Only when we took our walks did I feel at peace. Using my body physically was cathartic, as if I was somehow making up for how I'd shortchanged its potential to bring life into the world. I'd lost enough. And I knew I was losing Rob, too. I would not let my body wither away with everything else.

I didn't go back to college the next fall. Instead, I found a job at a stock brokerage firm and a cute mother-in-law unit to rent in Seattle. Shortly after Rob helped me move, we finally broke up. I lived alone and without him. I felt lost. Since right after the accident, he had been a major part of my life. Everything I had learned to do on one leg had been with Rob, and usually because of him. He had been my number one cheerleader, my advocate, my shoulder to cry on, my scapegoat. Rob had been my best friend—practically my only friend after high school. I had been so comfortable with him; he never judged me. I didn't have to worry about what he thought of me. Without him now, everything felt so hard. I was more afraid of what my future held than ever.

I needed to find something to lighten my heavy heart.

8

• ● •

CATCHING WIND

With Rob absent from my life, I had far too much time on my hands. And a person with an aching soul, an empty womb, and too much time on her hands is bound to do what she really needs to do: grieve. I couldn't risk going down that road. I needed to find a way to feel empowered. I needed something that would help me feel free from my limitations and connected to the greater world in some way, and maybe help me meet new people. I decided skiing would be just the thing. It's the only athletic activity I'd ever tried and liked before my accident.

One day, about three weeks after Rob and I broke up, I huddled over the enormous Seattle phone book, scanning the entries under *S*. Was there anyone out there, I dared hope, who could teach me how to ski? I remembered the joy and freedom two-legged skiing had given me as I sped down the slopes in seventh grade. I missed the joy of running, walking fast, riding a bike—anything that sent my hair whipping behind me. I yearned for speed. I had feelings to get away from, after all.

Ah! Here was something: "Skiforall: Instruction for disabled skiers." A bolt of excitement zipped through me as I envisioned myself skiing down a mountain. I called the number, desperately hoping this would be the answer. After a few minutes on the phone explaining my condition, they said yes, I qualified as disabled and could participate in their ski program. I signed up immediately, giddy with anticipation.

I was told I would ski without my prosthesis, which was big and heavy. I decided to wear my peg leg instead, which was lighter and more adaptable. A crude version of my prosthesis, it's basically a metal pylon with a rubber foot that screws into the socket I wear around my stump. But because the pylon lacks a knee unit, I walk like a stiff-legged pirate when I use it. While skiing, I would detach the pylon but leave the socket on to protect my stump from the cold and the falls.

On the first Sunday of lessons, I woke early after a fitful sleep. The night before, I'd gone to bed feeling like a child just before her first day of elementary school. My stomach swarmed with butterflies, and questions hounded my mind: *Who else will be skiing? What if I can't do it? What if I break my good leg?*

I was quite relieved to learn that Skiforall provided transportation for the disabled skiers. I avoided driving in the snow at all costs because it always made me feel panicky: bile flushed into my mouth, I broke into a cold sweat, and my knuckles turned white from wringing my hands. I didn't like my fear of driving in the snow, and yet it felt very justified.

I met the bus a half hour away from my Seattle home. I boarded the bus with the same nervousness I had in seventh grade when I first started riding school buses. My plan was to casually scan the aisle for the perfect bus partner: maybe a fun-looking woman or a cute guy. I climbed the steps one by one, already hot from all the clothes I was wearing. Inside the bus was loud and stuffy. As I scanned the nearly full seats, my heart dropped and heat rose to my face. Everyone there, except the chaperones, was mentally challenged. I was greeted by huge smiles and generous hellos.

"Take a seat where you can find one," said the bus driver.

Midway down the aisle, I found a seat with a happy-looking young woman who had the classic visage of a person with Down syndrome: slanted almond eyes and a flat nose.

"Ya wanna sit with me?" she asked, beaming at me.

"Thank you." I manually unlocked my knee, and it bent.

"I'm Cindy. What's your name?" she asked.

I had very little experience interacting with developmentally disabled people, so I wasn't sure how to talk to her.

"I'm Colleen," I said, feeling a huge wave of disappointment settle over me. I had been excited by the prospect of meeting a new community of people who were like me: *physically* disabled. I was incensed that the lady at the Skiforall office hadn't been clearer about my fellow passengers.

"Have you ever skied before?" Cindy asked, smiling. "This is my second year skiing, and last year I won two gold medals at the Skihawks. Coach Dan says I was the most improved last year. My friend Tina won three gold medals, but I was the most improved." Her pride was palpable.

"Really? Great. Good for you," I said, praising her like one might a child. I didn't want to be condescending, but I was caught off guard and was still trying to swallow the stone of disappointment lodged in my throat.

I glanced around the bus as Cindy continued talking about her skiing achievements. There were people, like Cindy, who clearly had Down syndrome. There were others whose heads bobbed steadily—who were quiet, their attention seemingly focused inward. Some were as young as ten; others looked as old as sixty. A chaperone from a few seats up looked at me with a friendly smile. I smiled back, feeling out of place where I sat, like being stuck on the visitor's side of the stadium at a home game—much like how I lived my whole life.

Cindy finished talking and started drawing smiley faces and flowers in the condensation covering the window. Her pictures looked like a first grader's. They made me smile, but not the smile one gives to a peer.

I felt guilty over my disappointment, but I had been hoping to get to know other amputees. I was desperate to know how other people dealt with their pain, anger, and frustration. I was gradually realizing that if I didn't have any role models, I could I never make progress on my own journey. The people on the bus were not my people. This wasn't what I had signed up for.

The noise level increased with each passing mile we climbed toward the pass. About halfway up, a chaperone stood up briefly and raised his hand, and the crowd quieted down.

"Let's keep it down, people. Hey, I know—let's give this bus driver a little incentive, shall we?" This was clearly a cue; instantly, the whole bus of people, seriously off-key, started singing "The Wheels on the Bus."

". . . go round and round, round and round, the wheels on the bus go round and round, up to the mountain . . ."

I sat with my arms crossed, smiling lamely. I knew I should be a good sport and join in, but I just wasn't up to it. I was feeling too discombobulated to make the best of the situation.

It took a little over an hour to get up to the pass, and I was exhausted. It was only eight thirty a.m., but I felt like I had lived a whole day already. My stomach flip-flopped as I realized it was time for the next phase of the adventure. One of the chaperones guided me to the rental office. Once there, a burly young guy with a head of curly brown hair came up to me.

"You must be here for the three-track ski lessons," he said. His eyes twinkled.

"Ummm, is that for amputees?"

"Yeah, it's called three-track 'cause you use outriggers on each arm and one ski. I'm Davin, and I'll be your instructor. You must be Colleen. The other two students are already here."

"Nice to meet you," I said, smiling. My disappointment was quickly dissipating. I hadn't expected a cute guy to be teaching me. Things were definitely looking up. I looked down and noticed he had two legs.

"So, you took the bus up. That must have been a wild ride, huh?" He was smiling, like he had taken the bus himself at some point. His smile was warm, not mocking.

"Yeah, it was wild."

He led me through the equipment rental process, where I was issued one boot, one ski, and two outriggers.

"Only the most accomplished one-legged skiers use ski poles," he explained. "They can rely solely on their one leg for balance. When you're learning, though, outriggers provide stability as you navigate down the mountain."

Outriggers, I learned, were the "amputee ski poles." Attached to the bottom of a waist-high metal pole is a mini ski, about twelve inches long. I would use a traditional ski on my good leg, giving me three "skis" to balance on, hence the term "three-track skiing." The top of the metal poles ended in metal armbands that fit around my forearms just below my elbows. My hands grasped the poles mid-way down; the handgrips stuck out like bike handles, though they faced forward instead of off to the side. Directly below the hand-grips were taut cotton strings that attached to the ski tips at the base of the poles. Davin demonstrated how it worked. He pulled up on the string, and the ski tip flipped up. A serrated edge on the back end of the ski provided traction, rendering the outrigger a crutch again, allowing me to get around the lodge or the flat areas outside. He pulled on the string again, put weight on the serrated edge, and the ski tip flipped back down so it could glide over the snow.

When I left the hospital five years ago, I used Canadian crutches, which were similar to outriggers, just without the ski tip, while I hobbled around waiting for my first prosthesis to be made. When I saw how the outriggers worked, I felt a little deflated, like I was taking a step backward. I didn't like the stigma or the inconvenience of crutches. I equated crutches with being poky. Little did I know how much they would help me fly.

I saw Davin's other students, two women, sitting farther down the bench in the crowded rental shop. They each had only one leg, too. On the bus ride up, all I could think about was wanting to meet other amputees, but seeing them sitting there, all I could think was, *No wonder people are compelled to stare at me.* Their stumps looked unnatural, even a little revolting. Like me, the other two amputees appeared to be in their early twenties. They were chatting quietly. I saw them occasionally look up at someone who was staring at them and return their gaze with a look I had given a million times over the years; the one that says, "Don't worry, I don't bite. I'm normal like you." The scene only made me wonder again if I'd done the right thing by coming up there.

After Davin made adjustments to my boot and I stowed the bottom half of my peg leg behind the rental desk, he made introductions.

"Linda and Becky, this is Colleen, the third musketeer!"

"Hi, I'm Linda. I hope ya'll know what you're doin', 'cause Becky and I are certain we're gonna be on our butts all day." Her velvety Southern accent warmed my heart immediately.

"Speak for yourself," said Becky good-naturedly. "I'm going to fly down the mountain and leave you in the dust." Linda smiled broadly.

"I don't know. I think I'll be on my butt with you, Linda," I said.

I was curious to know these women's stories, but Davin shepherded us into action before I could ask. Socializing would have to wait. We were in business mode.

Davin carried our skis as we crutched our way out to the snow. He set them down, one in front of each of us, and demonstrated how to step into the binding. We followed his instructions. Easy enough. Though Davin was wearing two ski boots, he used only one ski so he could demonstrate how we were to do things.

"Great! Now we're going to practice moving on these things. Follow me." He planted his outriggers into the snow, tips up in crutch form, pushed against them, and glided on his one ski. He kept his non-skiing leg bent. We all followed. The ground was fairly level, so this was easy. "Come on, keep going." People were watching us, smiles on their faces. Their enthusiasm and the sunny day made my heart leap with excitement. Maybe this would be okay. Maybe here on the mountain I would find just what I needed to get myself reoriented after leaving school and breaking up with Rob. There were other people in the world, after all. He wasn't the only person who could make me feel worthwhile.

Davin stopped. Directly in front of us was a slight slope. "Okay, ladies, let's start huffing up. I want you to be comfortable going down a hill before I take you up in a chairlift." He crutched up the incline with ease and speed. I followed, assuming I would be equally adept. This incline was smaller than a traditional bunny hill, yet I tired quickly. I planted my outriggers and slid my ski up to meet them. So I didn't lose ground, I quickly moved my outriggers farther up the incline—which was fast becoming a large hill—and rushed to push my ski forward to meet them.

"Damn, this is hard. I think I'd rather be on my butt!" Linda said, laughing at herself, which made me laugh. I had to stop and catch my breath before moving on. When we all met Davin at the top, we were huffing and puffing.

"Harder than it looks, isn't it? Don't worry, you'll get used to it. Okay, now comes the fun part. Watch how I use my outriggers for support, and the stance I use as I go down the hill."

Davin pulled on the outrigger strings, and the ski tips flipped down. He pushed off and headed down the hill, keeping his non-skiing leg bent. "Keep your knee slightly bent, ladies," he yelled as he turned his head uphill. "Keep your butt in. And relax."

It looked easy. The ground leveled out, and he eventually stopped. He flipped his ski tips up by pulling on the outrigger string and crutched back up the hill.

"Okay, now it's your turn. Go for it!"

I fumbled to find the string on my outrigger through my thick gloves. I pulled the string up, and my ski tips dropped flat. I started gliding before I was ready, and my ski leg got ahead of me. I fell down instantly. Becky fell down next to me, and we both started laughing. I was surprised at how hard this was, but it had been a long time since I'd laughed at myself. Davin showed us how to get up, which was another laborious physical task. Before I tried skiing again, I placed the outriggers slightly ahead of me. I glided down the hill, trying to remember to bend my knee. "Keep your butt in!" yelled Davin. I straightened my knee a little. "Good, now straighten your back!"

My hair wasn't blowing behind me as I'd envisioned when I signed up for these lessons, but I was skiing! I was giddy with delight. The slope eventually evened out, and I came to a stop. I found my outrigger strings, pulled on them, and my ski tips flipped up. I turned around and started hiking up the hill again. We all met at the top, and Davin gave us feedback about our form. When he demonstrated again, he made it look so easy.

After numerous times skiing down and hiking up, we finally mastered the anthill; a small success, but we were beaming and quite proud of ourselves. I, for one, felt a glorious lightness that I hadn't felt in years. Since the lesson had started, I hadn't felt guilty or angry or sorry for myself. The strenuous, physical effort I was putting in overshadowed the darker realities of my life.

"That was fun!" shrieked Becky.

"I can't imagine what a bona fide ski run will feel like." I squinted as I looked around for the next-highest hill, feeling a little nervous.

"Okay, so what's next?" asked Linda, looking around with me.

"Well, two-legged skiers would start with the rope tow," Davin explained, "but it's too difficult to navigate with your outriggers, so you're instantly graduating to the chairlift." Davin paused. "How many of you have been on a chairlift before?" Becky was the only one who hadn't. "Okay, Becky, I'll ride with you. Colleen and Linda, you ride together. We're going right over there to the smallest chairlift," he said, pointing to a lift off to our right. I followed the length of the lift up with my eyes, noting that it dumped out at the top of a small ridge. The hill we'd be skiing down was a beginner's hill, slightly steeper than a bunny hill, but for us one-legged newbies, it was the equivalent of a diamond-level expert's slope. I took a deep breath and exhaled slowly. *I can do this.*

Davin continued. "When we get there, I'll ask the lift operator to slow the lift waaaayyyy down. You'll plop your butt down on the chair and flip your outriggers to the ski position. Then when we get to the top, they'll slow it down again. When you get off the chair, just stand up and glide down the hill the same way we've just been doing. Any questions?"

Of course, we had a million of them. "What if I don't sit down in time?" "How do I hold my outriggers while I'm sitting?" "Do we stop at the top or just go straight down?" "What do we do if we drop an outrigger?" He patiently answered our questions until we were convinced we might actually be able to do this. "All right, ladies," he yelled, "let's ski!"

We were allowed to take cuts to the front of the line, which made me feel conspicuous, but I appreciated the perk; my right leg was starting to tire from standing on it for so long.

"So, you've skied before?" Linda asked me, as we slowly shuffled to the front of the line.

"Yeah, I was in seventh grade and had two legs then. What about you?"

"I was in grade school, before I had cancer. That's how I lost my leg." She was matter-of-fact.

"Oh. Wow." I was stunned into silence. I didn't know anyone who had survived cancer. I never thought about people losing their limbs that way. What was it like, I wondered, to know in advance it would happen? How did she and her parents make that decision? What was it like to go into surgery knowing you would come out with a part of your body missing? I wondered if I would have adjusted better to life with one leg if I'd had a little time to prepare instead of the way it had happened: one minute watching a green Pacer coming at me, the next minute watching my sister pointing at my leg, which was already separated from my body.

"Here comes the chair," Linda announced, pulling me away from my thoughts. The chairlift hummed as it slowed to a crawl. Davin and Becky simply plopped their butts down when the chair hit the back of their legs. That looked simple enough. Linda and I followed, crutching up to the red line that looked hazy under a layer of snow and ice. The chair slowly crept toward us. The lift operator courteously indicated when we were supposed to sit, which we did easily. I held onto the chair bar for dear life, remembering how much I didn't like heights. The nerve endings in my missing limb always went crazy, like when I moved a part of my body that had fallen asleep, only the feeling was a hundred times more intense.

"Don't forget to put your ski tips down," Linda reminded me, smiling.

Maneuvering the outrigger tips was much harder to do sitting down. We laughed nervously as we pressed them against our ski. The fir and hemlock trees, laden with snow, turned the hillside below into a winter wonderland.

"So, where do you live?" I asked.

"I live in Puyallup. How about you?"

Well, that's disappointing. She lives forty-five minutes from me. Too far away to get together for a quick lunch.

"I live in Seattle. So, what happens if we get stuck on this slope?" I laughed, but I wasn't entirely convinced I could get myself down the mountain on my own.

She laughed, too. "I was thinking the same thing. I suppose they could always call the ski patrol to get us down."

We crested a hill and saw the end of the lift just in front of us. Davin and Becky got off, and neither one of them fell. Linda and I scooted our butts forward as Davin had instructed, and we put our outriggers in the ready position. When we reached the top of the lift, Linda and I stood up to exit, and my stomach did a somersault. I did not want to fall while getting off! We tipped our skis down and glided down the short snowy ramp without eating it. We looked at each other with huge grins, unabashedly proud of ourselves. I felt like a little kid again, pleased with such a small accomplishment. We gathered as a group at the top of the lift and waited for Davin's instructions. Occasionally, someone looked at one of us and said, "Great job!" or "Good for you."

From where we stood above the slope, the hill looked long and steep. I felt like I was looking through the wrong end of a pair of binoculars.

"Okay, ladies, you can do this," Davin encouraged, a huge can-do smile on his face. "You're already skiers!" I felt myself enamored with his positive, supportive attitude. Since Rob, I hadn't really felt an attraction worth noting. This was a nice feeling.

Davin had us practice how to stop—by bearing weight on our ski so it swished perpendicular to the slope, stopping our descent. We started out slow, and it was surprisingly easy to stop. I felt like my leg naturally knew what to do, and though I thought the outriggers would be cumbersome, they were a godsend.

"Since you've all mastered stopping, I want you to take that same movement a step further and make it into a turn." As he demonstrated turning, I yearned to give it a try—more excited than scared—knowing I could do it. He gave us each a few opportunities to practice a turn on a small incline before the hill turned steep. Just as I thought, my body knew just what to do. Becky and Linda were naturals, too. The three of us were concentrating and trying hard. This was the first time since the accident I had shared a physical success with someone in my situation. It wasn't like going on a hike with Rob, where I always had to keep up. I wasn't keeping up with these women; I was one of them. All of a sudden, I felt a new kind of normal.

"Ladies, let's ski down the mountain!" Davin announced excitedly. "I'm right here, following you the whole way. The left side of the run has a gentler slope, so we're going to stick to that side."

We all looked at each other, waiting to see who would go first. Once we were at this juncture, we were all scared. I wanted to get it over with, so I scooted my ski tip downhill and pushed off. I gained speed immediately. I was going so fast, I couldn't think about what to do. "Turn, Colleen, turn!" Davin called from behind me. I could hear Becky and Linda whooping and hollering, and the next thing I knew, I was on my butt, sliding down the hill, embarrassed and disappointed. Davin quickly skied down to me. "Way to go!" he encouraged. "Now, on your next try, keep your butt in, straighten your back, and carve a turn."

I reached a hand up, hoping he would help me.

"Sorry, but you're on your own. You remember how to get up, right? I'm not always going to be right here, so you gotta get used to it. Believe me, after today, you'll be a pro at getting back up."

"Thanks a lot. That's a true vote of confidence," I said with a smile and an edge of sarcasm.

"Well, I always tell my students, you're not learning if you're not falling."

Davin left to crutch back up the hill to Becky and Linda, and I managed to get back up. I was sweating by the time I got up, so I took off my hat and stuffed it in my jacket pocket.

I waited for Becky and Linda to take their turns; they fell, too. We all ended up in roughly the same place and regrouped for another pep talk from Davin.

"Okay, you're all doing the same thing. Get those butts in, ladies. Stay relaxed. And this time, carve a turn. Show me what you can do!"

Davin was clearly an expert at teaching three-track skiing, so if he said I could do it, I believed him. He reminded me of Anne, my physical therapist, and the confidence she had in me. His words energized me. I pointed my ski downhill and pushed off. I attempted a turn right away, so I didn't gain speed too quickly. With my knee bent, I bore weight on my heel and turned my knee hillside. *Whoosh!* I did it. I made a turn. I felt a rush of relief and joy.

"Go, baby, go!" Davin yelled. The other girls were yelling, too. I looked up and smiled at them as I traversed the hillside. I fell again. Laughing at myself, I lay in the snow for half a minute and felt the expansiveness of my chest, ready to burst from the glow of happiness, before I hoisted myself back up. Linda was now coming down, but she immediately fell.

It took us a full hour to get down the run. If Rob were here, I would have been snapping at him in frustration every time I fell, but there was no one there I could take out my frustration on. Instead, I managed each fall as it came, taking a short rest and then hoisting myself up. I started to recognize able-bodied skiers who, during the course of my one trip down the run, had taken multiple trips down. Many of them were encouraging; some asked if I needed help getting up. I always refused. Davin was right: I needed to get used to getting up on my own. Others cheered me on as I practiced a turn. "Great job!" I heard often. Their comments felt good, because I recognized what I was doing was hard and novel. When I'd last skied ten years before, I never saw a one-legged skier.

Linda, Becky, and I offered each other encouragement all the way down: "Way to go! You can do it!" "Woo-hoo, look at you!" "You're doing great!" Those were the most valuable words I heard all day, because they knew just how hard this was—not just the skiing itself, but putting ourselves out here in the first place, in spite of feeling self-conscious or different. We gave one another courage.

As the afternoon wore on, we did several more runs, and I imprinted on my brain how to make the turns, how to bend my knee, and how to get up after falling down. There was an old body memory from when I skied in seventh grade resurfacing on my way down each run. I skied long enough and gained enough speed to send my hair whipping behind me.

My heart was nearly bursting. I found myself skiing—truly skiing—fast enough so the wind whistled in my ears. And I felt no pain. No phantom pain. No pain from my prosthesis rubbing against my stump. The only pain I felt was on my butt, from falling down so much.

A whole new world was opening up to me. I had just been told I could do anything. And at least on that day I believed it.

9

SOCCER

Learning to ski revealed how free my body felt without my prosthesis attached. There was such joy in movement unencumbered by the "ball and chain." My body's movements were lighter. Even crutching uphill using my outriggers, I felt unchained; there was something pure about the movement. In essence, I felt a renewed connection to my body.

But as pure and free as I felt when I was on the mountain, I still daily fought the sense that I was an outsider in a world where people seemed to understand one another. The trial was behind me, but the anguish of hearing someone blame me for my accident lingered. And the blame I'd heaped on myself after the abortion was often present as well. My craving for a connection with others who might understand and validate me was like a visceral yearning.

I was disappointed I didn't become better friends with Becky or Linda. We never socialized off the mountain. They were nice women, but we didn't really click. So while I achieved part of what I wanted through skiing—an understanding of how I could use my body—I didn't achieve the social connection I was seeking. I knew there were people out there who I could relate to, who could understand me; I just hadn't found them yet.

To manage my loneliness, and to avoid the anger I felt continually brewing under the surface, I made a not-quite-conscious decision to throw myself into as many physical activities as I could. Maybe if I poured myself into risk-taking, I could make myself into someone I could admire—someone others would want to connect with.

Always a lover of saltwater and intrigued by the idea of exploring its depths, I signed up for scuba-diving lessons. I was excited to swim in the Puget Sound and discover her treasures. Unfortunately, the four weeks of classroom instruction were boring, and I was disappointed when the class offered only two dives. And while the experience of scuba diving had its own pleasures—the feeling of my body undulating in water, the weights counterbalancing the fat on my stump, watching fish swim by—scuba diving ultimately wasn't for me. The equipment felt too cumbersome and was difficult to transport without wearing my prosthesis. Besides, scuba diving is a partner sport, and I didn't have anyone in my life who was interested in it. Everyone else in the class had a partner. And while they all admired me and were very kind, I felt distanced from them, like I was from a foreign country. I was on the outside of the group knocking to get in, but they just wouldn't answer the door. Though I was successful at the scuba diving itself, I wasn't successful at making new friends among divers.

Skydiving was the next activity to catch my interest. Since I lived with fear every day of my life—fear of needing to get out of the way of a moving car faster than I could walk, for example—I thought the rush of skydiving might push me beyond it. I jumped out of an airplane at three thousand feet and prayed to God my chute would open. The thrill of the moment was overwhelming and satisfying but ultimately empty. And it was a lot of work for a short-lived rush. Plus, again, there were no relationships to be had in the amateur skydiving community.

Skiing seemed to be my sport—the best chance for me to both excel athletically and meet people with similar challenges to mine—so the next year, I was back at the mountain taking classes with Davin and improving my skills. At the end of my second ski season, Davin introduced me to Don, a fifty-five-year-old, silver-haired amputee.

One day after a particularly good run, several of us were sitting in the lodge unwinding when Don said to me, "Hey, we gotta get you on the soccer field. Why don't you come play soccer with the amputee soccer team?"

I didn't even know what he was talking about. "How do amputees play soccer?" I asked.

"We take our legs off and hop around on our crutches. Come on, it's a great workout and a lot of fun. We need more girls on the team."

I couldn't really picture what a field full of amputees kicking around a soccer ball would look like, but since I'd made a commitment to throw myself into physical activity, I reluctantly agreed to try. My brothers had played soccer, so I had a cursory understanding of the object of the game. And while I wasn't burning with desire to kick a ball around, I *was* itching to spend more time with people who might understand me and the complexity of my life. I so much wanted to belong somewhere.

On my first day as a soccer player, I woke up at six a.m. and drove the half hour to the indoor soccer field. I walked in and saw about ten artificial legs leaning against the wall outside the field. My heart both leapt in excitement at being among so many other one-legged people, and cinched up in fear at being expected to make my way across a soccer field without my prosthetic.

"Hey, there she is!" Don said. I felt out of my realm. I looked around and saw a lot of guys, some quite a bit younger than Don; and if there was one group of people I was especially anxious around, it was men my own age. As I slipped off my leg, Don explained the rules for playing on crutches. What he didn't understand was that I lacked an understanding of even the most basic rules of soccer. All I knew was each team tried to kick the ball into the net. Off sides, fouls, and penalty kicks all meant nothing to me.

"Don, I don't really know what you're talking about," I offered sheepishly. "I've never played soccer before."

"Never?" he asked, looking surprised.

"No, never," I said, laughing nervously, not sure if he would let me play.

"Well, there's always a first, right?" He gave me a brief overview of the game in a kind, fatherly way, and we both decided I would learn as I went.

I didn't know soccer could be so vicious. On more than one occasion, I was slammed into the wall as my opponent rammed into me to take possession of the ball. The first time it happened, I stopped dead in my tracks, not understanding why he'd purposely hurt me. The man who had done it, deftly move the ball back to his net while laughing, just like my brothers would have done. Tears sprang to my eyes.

Rashid, one of my teammates, a cute, curly-haired guy from Lebanon, came over to me.

"Don't worry, he didn't mean anything. Indoor soccer can be a lot more physical than outdoor soccer." His smooth accent and deep-brown eyes took my mind off my hurt feelings.

The game ended, and we all left the field to get our legs. Rashid hopped over to mine.

"Is this yours?" he asked.

"Yes." I answered, blushing. He picked up my leg easily and hopped it over to me, his curls bouncing with each hop.

My leg is private. I don't let just anyone touch it. In its own way, my prosthesis had become a part of my body—a part of my "self" in a way I couldn't have named. And there he was, carrying it over to me and handing it to me like a perfect gentleman handing a bouquet of flowers to a proper lady on their first date. The blush I felt in my face must have revealed how my heart was melting when he handed me my leg.

"Thank you," I mustered with a throaty whisper.

"You're welcome," he answered with casual confidence, like handing a woman her leg was what a gentleman was supposed to do.

The team often went out to breakfast after our games, which was the part of being a soccer player I liked best. It was at one of these breakfasts that I learned Rashid had been in the States for five years. He'd come for "some surgeries" and decided to stay. I was all ears during the conversation that morning, waiting to hear what I wanted to know, but Rashid skirted the issue of how he'd lost his leg in Lebanon.

He did tell us that he'd been playing soccer since he was a boy. "I am so happy to be able to kick a ball around again," he said, and heads nodded all around our breakfast table.

Why didn't he just say it all? I wondered. We all knew the pain. We could all relate. We could all offer support and comfort if only he would open up. I felt frustrated, as I had before, that people were so reluctant to tell their stories. Later, when I heard of how he'd stepped on a land mine during the Lebanese civil war, I knew I had no real basis for understanding the painful part of his tragedy, which involved living through a war and leaving his homeland.

Maybe I was trying too hard to find common places to commiserate with others. In order to understand what had happened to me, I wanted to talk to people who knew, intimately, what it felt like to lose a literal part of themselves. My soccer friends all seemed to be thriving without a need to talk about their losses. In fact, they seemed to be masters at not talking about it, at subtly evading the issue.

I wanted to tell my story to someone who could understand, hoping the shared experience would help me find some relief from the sadness I felt. But my friends didn't want to probe me about my loss any more than they wanted me to probe them about theirs. They didn't seem to care about the past; they seemed only to care about their next thrill.

I wasn't good at soccer, but I was thrilled at the notion that I could play. I stayed on the team for one whole season, reveling in my bond with other amputees, the smell of a dirty locker room, the thrill of a teammate making a goal, the after-game play-by-play at breakfast, and the snap of a towel on my butt that let me know I was a part of a team.

I was twenty-three, and for the first time in my life, I was able to attach a positive label to myself. In just six years, my self-image had changed so drastically. And although there was still so much angst and grief under the surface, I was able to admit that, ironically, I'd gained something by losing my leg. I never would have pursued these activities if I still had my leg. I never would have questioned what my body could do. A whole new world was opening up to me that begged me to challenge myself in ways I never would have dreamed.

And then, my world broke open even wider: Davin asked me to join the ski team the following winter, and I accepted. After soccer season was over, I would spend every weekend running gates and learning how to race on one leg. I would live with my hair whipping in the wind behind me.

10

• ● •

BOGUS BASIN

Competing on the ski team would give me the final push I needed to get me back to school.

On my first day of actual racing, breathing heavily from my hike up the hill, I glided into my gate. A horizontal bar, waist high, kept me from quickly descending onto the course. The air announced itself in small puffs with each nervous breath I took. From behind me, the crowd hooted and hollered for the skier currently tackling the course. I didn't dare look at her. I focused on my red-and-black ski boot, reviewing the course in my mind, remembering how I had skied down the hill numerous times the day before, parallel to the course, echoing each turn as if the gates were in front of me. I felt I knew the course, I just hadn't run it yet. The weather was cold here at Bogus Basin, Idaho, and there was no fresh snow. Many racers had skied the track already, each one etching a deeper groove into the course.

Davin, who was now my coach, stood behind me. I felt his warm breath on a small exposed area of my neck as he offered words of encouragement, "Okay, relax and take it easy. This is supposed to be fun!" I grasped my outriggers, pumped my leg a few times to warm it up, took some deep breaths, and waited for the gun's pop to announce my turn.

As I waited, it was not lost on me that in less than three years, since the abortion and since breaking up with Rob, I had found

enough physical strength and emotional independence to believe
I might, possibly, be okay. I still lived in the same mother-in-law
apartment in Seattle and still worked at my full-time job at the stock
brokerage firm, but I had enough sense of self now to feel that my
life was going somewhere. I still carried around a boulder of anger
at Harvey and, now, at the insurance companies and at the juror
who had blamed me for my accident, but whenever I thought about
it, I focused on making my body work hard . . .

Pop! The gun went off and I was flying down the hill, hair waving
behind me. My first race!

The Seattle contingent of disabled skiers, which I was a part of,
had traveled en masse to Bogus Basin for our ski competition. Our
small plane had been filled to capacity with physically disabled skiers of every kind: paraplegic, quadriplegic, hemiplegics, amputees
(both of the arms and legs), vision impaired, and hearing impaired.
Some were a part of my team from Snoqualmie Pass, where I'd first
learned to ski with Linda and Becky; the remainder were from other
Western Washington ski areas. We'd kept the flight attendants busy
on the hour-long flight by quickly gulping our beers and ordering
more. We were loud, proud, and obnoxious. As we approached our
destination, I sat back in my seat and felt the sense of belonging, at
least for the moment, that I was always seeking.

But traveling with a bunch of folks in wheelchairs brought home
the reality of a life I had been spared. Had Harvey's car hit me with
a little more force, my right leg would have been taken from me as
well. Had I been hit a few inches higher, I would likely be paralyzed
from the waist down. These people I was traveling with required
varying degrees of help, from transfers to and from their chairs to
carrying their equipment.

Once in Bogus Basin, Linda, Becky, and I were roommates. We
shared our room with a woman Becky knew, Theresa, who was a
Thalidomide baby: a child born from a mother who took this drug

in the 1960s, which caused serious birth defects. Theresa had been born with four seal-like appendages instead of arms and legs. Her vibrant smile and quick wit enchanted me, but her disability riveted me and made me consider my own struggle. During the days we shared a room, I watched her surreptitiously from the corner of my eye as she maneuvered her abbreviated body around the queen-sized bed. Quick, agile, and surprisingly adept, she held her shirt under her flipper-like arm and wriggled her body into it. Even her neck seemed to have muscles mine didn't. She clearly had accommodated her limited arms and legs years ago. I held the same awe and reverence for her that able-bodied people who had come to know me since my accident often felt for me. What I lived with was nothing compared to what Theresa lived with, but I gained something by watching her: the message that limitations were as much in the mind as in the body.

Getting dressed in the morning in front of Linda, Becky, and Theresa wasn't uncomfortable like it was when I was around two-legged friends. Instead of feeling like the freak in the room, I was able to openly watch my roommates put on their prosthetic legs and ask questions about them. But I still wanted so much to broach the subject of anger and pain with someone who might get it, and I didn't know how. I longed to talk about what I felt like were my false hopes about marriage and children. I didn't want to appear prying, and I understood that such topics were personal, but I desperately needed to know how these other women were grappling with these issues.

After one full day of skiing, we all headed back to the lodge. Inside, it was littered with outriggers and artificial legs leaning against the walls. Ski parkas and hats were scattered across the long, picnic-style tables. The vaulted room was stuffy and hot, the windows steamy from all the body heat. I found space at a crowded table with Linda and Becky, anxious as usual to make the kind of connections that were continually elusive to me. These were my people, but I felt separate nonetheless.

A young, handsome guy with piercing blue eyes in a wheelchair was sitting at the table, too. "Hey, I haven't met you before. What's your name?" he said.

"I'm Colleen. What about you?"

"I'm Gary, and I'm gonna kill the run tomorrow," he said, pounding his fist on the table.

Okay, so he's had a few, I thought. But I could put the slurring of words aside for a good-looking young man.

Gary and I quickly discovered we skied on different days up at Snoqualmie and that we were both equally passionate about skiing. We filled the next hour drinking beer and talking of snow conditions, how the course would run the next day, and of new equipment coming onto the market.

"So, how'd ya lose it?" Gary asked suddenly, his voice quieter.

"A car accident," I said, feeling self-conscious but hopeful that I was on the edge of talking to someone honestly about how they really dealt with their daily struggles—their anger, their physical pain. Here was my chance to steer a conversation into the more intimate space I longed to go. But I couldn't think of what to say next. So I was silent, afraid the moment would be lost.

"Rough," said Gary. He abruptly turned away from me to Davin, as if to avoid further discussion on the topic. "Hey, coach, are you going to get me another beer, or do I hafta run over you?"

"I'm making a run. Just sit there nice and pretty, Gary." Other folks yelled their orders to Davin as he walked toward the bar.

"I expect a good tip, people." Davin yelled through his dimpled smile.

I nursed my beer, chastising myself for hoping for more than I was likely to get from a casual conversation, and for choking up in the face of an opportunity for a meeting of the minds with Gary. I decided to skip it for the moment.

But after a few beers, I was bold enough to ask Gary how he broke his back. "Vietnam," he said in a clipped tone.

"Oh, wow, what happened?" I asked naively.

"Oh, I don't talk about the war." Then he turned his torso in his chair and started a conversation with another paraplegic behind him.

I finished my beer, got up, and crutched out into the cold, dark night. The air bit my face. I felt stupid for asking so bluntly about the war. I should have been more sensitive. I felt embarrassed that I had tried to open up his world a little and had been met with a slammed door. Mostly, in that moment I felt sad for him, sad that this part of his life was so concealed, so hidden, simply not talked about. In fact, I felt sad that so many people didn't talk about what had happened to them, even to those of us who could best empathize. It would be years later when I would finally understand that not talking about something didn't mean that someone was running from that thing. I couldn't see it then, because for me, I was running—or skiing—away from the shadow part of me.

In spite of some continuing sense of not quite perfectly fitting in anywhere, I was strong enough to move forward. I decided to move to Bellingham and to go back to college the next fall. As a result, I would lose touch with the many of the people with whom I'd spent the past three years. I'd had fun with them and learned from them how to show up, live in the moment, and use my body to its fullest potential. Though I'd never had the opportunity to talk about my deepest feelings with them, I did now understand that what we each went through with our disability was deeply personal, almost too personal to talk about sometimes. Had we talked about the emotions, it may have caused us too much pain. Instead we modeled for each other how to be positive; we buoyed each other in a sea of possibility; we taught one another that our disabilities were only as hard as we made them.

11

UNFORGIVABLE

I received the call in the early-morning hours.

"Hello?" I said, a pit forming in my stomach. I had inherited Mom's fear of middle-of-the-night phone calls.

"Colleen, everything's fine," Mom reassured me. I breathed a sigh of relief, happy to hear her voice. If everything was fine, her call could only mean one thing. "It's a boy!" she said excitedly. "Molly had the baby. He was born just about an hour ago."

I sat up in bed and rearranged my covers. The lilt in Mom's voice gave away her delight at her first grandchild's birth. A big smile came to my face. I was flushed with excitement, too.

"How is everybody doing?" I asked. My sister-in-law, Molly, had been on bed rest for the past six weeks for something I didn't really understand.

"Everyone's doing well. There were no problems. He has ten fingers and ten toes. His name is Brendon."

"That's great, Mom. How long will they be in the hospital?" I was trying to figure out how to rearrange my schedule so I could drive the two hours to see him. Then I said, "Oh, wait, today is Sunday. I can come down today!" My heart skipped a beat in excitement when I realized I could see my first nephew on his first day of life.

"Wonderful. Just call before you leave."

"Okay, *Grandma*, I will," I said in a joking tone. Mom had discussed at length how she didn't like the title of grandma. Although she didn't have an alternative yet, she at least knew her grandchildren wouldn't be calling her that.

"Oh, stop!" she said through her laughter. "I love you, honey."

"I love you, too, Mom."

On the two-hour drive to Bellevue, I was surprised at how nervous I was to be around a baby. During the drive, I smoked more cigarettes than usual. After an hour and a half of driving, an image of Molly going through labor flashed through my mind. I couldn't help but remember myself in stirrups having my baby vacuumed out of me. I let out a gasp, old emotions flooding through me, and I suddenly burst into tears. I sent out a silent prayer to the child I'd given up: *I'm so sorry, little one. I'm sorry. Wait for me till I'm ready.*

At the hospital, looking for Molly's room, the familiar antiseptic odor held a different memory, filling me with dread. I had both fond and horrid memories of being in the hospital after my accident. I loved my physical therapist and the nurses, but I hated all the pain I experienced and how my accident had forever changed my life. I took a deep breath and wiped away the tears before knocking on Molly's door.

Mom opened the door, a little bundle of white cotton in her arms.

"Come in," she said in a hush, retreating back into the room. Molly was in bed. My brother Kevin was sitting in a chair next to her, holding her hand. My mom's new husband, Larry, was sitting in the corner reading a magazine. I was intrigued to see my mother hold a baby. She was so confident, so strong, and she oozed Mama Bear energy. Is that what I would look like as a mother? I walked up to look at Brendon sleeping in Mom's arms. "Ooooohhhh, he's so tiny," I remarked. My breath became shallow.

The room was uncharacteristically quiet for my family. As I gave my hugs, hellos, and congratulations, everyone spoke in whispers. I was shown the sink and instructed to wash my hands before holding the baby. Kevin and Molly looked tired and were softly talking to Mom and Larry about lunch plans as I washed my hands. I walked over to Mom and stood in front of her swaying body.

"Do you want to hold him?" she asked. I nodded my head tentatively and held out my hands.

"Why don't you sit down to hold him, honey." I walked over to the plastic rendition of an easy chair, sat down, took a deep breath, and held out my arms. Mom placed Brendon in my arms and slid her arms out from under mine. He was wrapped tightly in a soft cotton blanket, with just his head and upper chest exposed.

He was so light. He barely weighed an ounce. I couldn't believe his skin, so pure and white. His eyelashes were tiny and blond; I could see the veins in his eyelids. His diminutive hands were folded, as if in prayer, against his chest. The weight in my chest felt like love and sadness all at once. My throat constricted and seared with pain. Tears filled my eyes. *Is this what I gave up? What would my son have looked like? How horrible am I that I snuffed out one of these? My baby would be almost four years old by now.*

I looked up at Molly and Kevin. "He's beautiful," I whispered, almost too overwhelmed to speak. I knew they could see my tears. Were they more than what was appropriate? Were they confusing to them? I couldn't hold them back. I just let them flow. Brendon was so beautiful, so incredibly angelic.

I'm so sorry. God, I'm so sorry, I said inside my heart. My faith, faded though it had been in recent years, lived ever-present just under the surface of my awareness. Though there were days when I seriously questioned whether there was a God, at this moment, I was sure I was in the presence of the sacred.

Brendon started wriggling and making noises, and I didn't know what to do. I looked at Mom in a panic. Taking my cue, she said, "Here, let me give him to Molly. He might be getting hungry."

I sat still, reeling from my few moments with Brendon. I wanted to keep holding him, but he scared me. How could something so little scare me? Then I remembered how my eight-week-old fetus had scared the shit out of me. Small things can be very scary.

Brendon was born on December 2nd. I had finals and end-of-the-quarter papers to write. Back at school, after my tender day with Brendon, I was melancholy, and the familiar sadness I had lived with since the abortion returned full force. After Rob and I broke up, I stayed in Seattle and worked at the stock brokerage firm. I'd taken three years off before going back to school to finish my degree and thought I was doing well now. But in the aftermath of what was such a miraculous event for my brother, for my family, I was alone in my sadness all over again. That day with Brendon had put a chink in my carefully crafted Super Girl armor, allowing the sadness I usually kept in check a tiny escape route. I longed to talk about this sadness. I had been back at school for a little over a year by this time, but I hadn't developed any close friendships. The people closest to me, my family, had no idea I had had an abortion. I had told only a few friends back when it had happened, but in their minds, it was long over—no big deal.

I agreed to spend the two weeks of my Christmas break with Kevin and Molly in Bellevue, helping with the baby. After a grueling week of finals, I packed my bag and headed south.

Molly had married my brother only ten months prior, and I didn't know her very well. Kevin was at work all day, which allowed time for Molly and me to get to know each other through this lens of motherhood. While she was learning how to be one, I was learning what I gave up.

I learned babies don't sleep when we want them to. Because she was nursing, Molly bore the brunt of Brendon's irregular sleeping pattern. I was a deep sleeper, so I usually slept through the middle-of-the-night feedings. I woke up each morning to make Kevin his coffee as he got ready for work. If Brendon woke up, I held him and kept him quiet for as long as I could so Molly could sleep. I followed Molly's lead and swayed back and forth, dotting each rocking motion with tiny bounces. I kissed his nose and his toes, surprised at my natural ability to hold and care for this infant. My first few days with Brendon were accompanied by an ache in my heart. I was afraid it would explode and expose the truly horrible person I was to have given up an opportunity for all this. But I felt like Brendon was protecting me from a full-on emotional crash. Looking into his face caused this ache, but his innocent, beguiling stares back at me took away the pain.

I loved diving into his endlessly deep-blue eyes. He reminded me of an old man, with years of accumulated wisdom. Brendon just stared at me as if he held a secret. I searched, wondering if he knew the soul I'd snuffed out. *Did you know him? Did you talk to him? Is he mad at me?* I whispered to him when we were alone. I felt silly wondering this, but Brendon felt like he was still a part of God's world, still attached to heaven.

Molly didn't leave the house often, but on one occasion, when she left Brendon in my care for an hour, he had a crying fit. No amount of rocking and swaying helped. I didn't have a bottle to give him since he was nursing, and he didn't want his pacifier. I remembered seeing Kevin maneuver Brendon during similar crying fits. I tried some of his moves: turning him facedown with his stomach over my forearm, lifting him up in the air above my head, patting his back with more force than seemed appropriate for a baby. Nothing worked. Brendon's howls intensified. I started crying, too. "Please stop. Please just stop now." I begged and pleaded, and this wise little baby turned into a menace, taunting me, showing me what a horrible mother I would have been. I couldn't even comfort a crying baby. I ping-ponged from feeling guilty to thinking, *It's a good thing I gave up motherhood. I would have been a lousy mother.*

The day before I was to go back to college for winter quarter, we were all sitting in the living room. Molly was on the couch holding Brendon, and Kevin was sitting next to her, sipping coffee. I sat across from them noticing how they looked like the perfect family. *Will I ever have that?* I silently lamented, just beginning to feel again the yearning for a family of my own, which I thought I'd long ago dismissed as a possibility.

"Colleen, Molly and I want to ask you something." Kevin put his arm around Molly's shoulder.

"Sorry, guys, I can't stay any longer," I joked. "I have to get back to school." We all laughed. Although we all knew I was kidding, a huge part of me wanted to stay in this baby bubble. Time slowed down here.

"Actually, we'd like you to be Brendon's godmother." Kevin eyes twinkled and looked into mine.

I gasped. My heart started racing. I had a million questions. "What does that mean?"

"Well, we know you don't go to church much anymore . . ." I flushed with guilt hearing him speak so openly about what I had never admitted to the family. Because being Catholic was such a huge part of my family's identity, I'd simply stopped talking about church and hoped that no one had noticed. "But we feel like you're a very spiritual person. We want you to be able to share your beliefs and values with Brendon." *Really? Me? But I'm such a louse. If you knew what I'd done, you wouldn't be asking me this.* There was no way I could reveal my secret, though, especially to Kevin and Molly, and especially now that they had a precious baby. Then something stirred in me. From beyond the deep, remorseful, dark place within me came a small voice, reminding me I did have value and goodness to give. I had been finding my own way spiritually, trying to form a new relationship with God that made sense to me. And as a person learning to live life with one leg, perhaps I did have something of strength and resilience to share with this little guy.

"I'd be honored," I said through my tears. I looked over at Molly, holding my godson, *my* godson, and I smiled. I walked over to the couch, sat next to Molly, and the four of us hugged.

Brendon's baptism was a month later, at the same church in which I was baptized. During the ceremony I felt proud to hold this place of honor on the altar, sharing this moment with Kevin and his family.

But I couldn't ignore the pit growing in my stomach, leaving me hollow. I had to force myself not to fall into the abyss of guilt and sadness. If I had been alone in the church with God, I would have thrown myself on the altar and begged his forgiveness. Whether I fully believed in him or not, Catholicism was the only path I knew for making amends for sin. But I stood still. The church was full of smiling, happy people, so I steeled myself behind my armor and smiled along, willing my eyes to sparkle instead of cry.

The gnawing guilt followed me back to Bellingham. Since I had no one to talk to, I found myself ruminating and condemning myself for the abortion instead of studying. I spent long hours wondering about what my own baby would have been like instead of writing my papers.

One morning I woke up and knew that I needed to make this right with God. I had never been to confession for my sin of abortion. True, I hadn't been attending mass often, but I grew up a good Catholic girl, and I figured I had earned the right to talk to a priest. I decisively called up the local Catholic church and made an appointment. I needed to move past this guilt, and the only way I knew how to was to seek God's healing.

A few days later, I was sitting on a small couch in the rectory, waiting for the priest to arrive. A comfortable plaid easy chair was waiting for him, too. Shelves were littered with ecumenical books, and plaques with bible quotes lined the walls: "Blessed be the meek, for they shall inherit the earth." "For God so loved the world that he gave his only son." The room smelled heavy with the scent of age and old incense. My hands were sweaty, so I kept wiping them on my jeans in case he shook my hand when we met. My heart was racing. *Can I really confess? Can I really tell him what I did?*

The door opened quickly, and he ambled in. He was balding and wearing glasses. He smelled like Ivory soap. His jowls hung over a black-and-white collar. Yep, he was every inch the parish priest.

"Hello, Colleen." He offered his hand, and I shook it, hoping mine wasn't too sweaty.

"Hello, Father Dempsey. Thank you for seeing me." My shaking voice gave away my nerves. I resisted the tears, wishing this feeling would go away. I paced inside myself, like a caged animal.

"We're lucky to have such a beautiful day in January, aren't we?" Father Dempsey said.

What? We're going to chitchat? I thought I'd just blurt out my confession.

"Yes, we are." My feeble smile gave away my discomfort. I looked around the room.

He looked right at me. His eyes were soft, but not as kind as I needed. "What can I do for you, Colleen?"

"I, um, I want to make a confession." I swallowed hard. I wiped my hands on my jeans.

"Yes, whenever you're ready."

"Four years ago, well, um . . ." The words didn't want to come out. I hadn't told many people, and it didn't feel right to use the word "abortion" in association with me. "I had . . . I had an abortion." I hung my head in shame. Dread enveloped me. I was scared shitless now that I'd told him. What would he say? I desperately wanted him to come over and hug me and tell me I wasn't a piece of crap. I wanted him to live out the Christian values of forgiveness and compassion that were heralded around the cluttered room in books and art.

"I see." Silence.

Unbearable silence.

"I was twenty years old," I said, needing to fill the space, which in itself felt so accusatory and scornful. I needed him to understand why. "I had lost my leg a few years before, and I was in school, and I just couldn't have the baby." I was crying now and trying desperately not to. I could hardly talk because my throat was closing up, like it wanted me to just shut up.

He handed me a tissue. He didn't say a word. I wiped my eyes and my nose and looked up at him. "What can I do to be forgiven?"

"In the eyes of God, Colleen, abortion is an unforgivable sin." He sat in his chair like a statue, unmoving. His eyes turned hard. I had to look away.

My heart started beating wildly, and a combination of terror and rage started to rise from my stomach into my throat. *What the fuck is he talking about?* I thought I was supposed to be able to confess my sins and be forgiven. I'd pushed through some significant doubts and real reservations to make this appointment, trusting that, though I had not been practicing regularly, my childhood faith would still be there for me if I returned to it. Now I was learning that what I had done was completely, utterly unforgivable. I'd never heard this before. Didn't even inmates on death row receive forgiveness for their heinous crimes if they repented? I looked back at him. His hands were together, fingertip to fingertip, just under his chin. His eyes were unchanged. My heart was completely broken.

"Colleen, I understand this isn't what you want to hear, but . . ." I couldn't hear anything else he said. We talked about fifteen minutes more, but I don't remember a word. While he was talking to me about the church and God and Jesus, I was thinking about how I just wanted to run the hell out of that room. I wanted to get in my car and have a cigarette. I just wanted to go back to my house and light up a joint and disappear from the pain I was carrying in my chest cavity. I replied to whatever he said to me during those minutes, but I couldn't give voice to what I really wanted to say. I couldn't slap him across the face like I wanted to because even now, sitting unforgiven across from this cruel man, I was still a good Catholic girl.

"Colleen, I have another appointment coming in a few minutes. Shall you and I schedule another appointment so we can talk about this some more?" He reached over to grab his black leather calendar as if there were no question I'd say yes.

"Sure." *Not one chance in hell.* We set up the appointment, and I wondered if he knew, as strongly as I did, that we wouldn't be meeting again.

I couldn't walk out of his office fast enough. Once I was outside the rectory, I gasped for fresh air, for relief, and I started to bawl. *Keep it together till you get to the car, Goddamn it.* But I couldn't. The floodgates had burst, and I was along for the ride. I couldn't get to my car quickly enough. Through my tears, my mouth watered at the thought of a cigarette. My hands were shaking so much I had trouble grasping the keys at the bottom of my purse. When I got inside my car, I uncharacteristically locked the doors. I didn't want him to be able to come after me. I didn't want anything Catholic to seep into my car. I drove away as fast as I could. I was crying too much to have a cigarette, so I just drove to the closest beach.

I got out of the car and walked quickly to the water's edge. The wind blew over me like a spring shower. The seagulls hung suspended in the air like kites. I kept wiping away the tears for what felt like an eternity, until finally they slowed down. I didn't have any tissues and cursed my nose for running so much. I had to wipe it on my sleeve. I sat down on the rocky shore and had my cigarette. With each drag, I settled into my body a little more. With each puff, my breathing evened out, and though I was completely unconscious of it at the time, I made a vow to get through the end of my quarter and throw myself back into life the best I could.

12

• • •

ANOTHER CHOICE

My older sister Mary Beth had her first child a year after Brendon was born, the second grandchild in the family. I was so happy for her yet so unhappy for myself. In the "normal" lives of my siblings, who were getting married and starting families, I saw exactly what was elusive to me. Rob hadn't loved me enough to marry me, I told myself, and I had terminated a pregnancy rather than celebrated my child's birth. I just felt like I couldn't do life right. Not for the first time—or even for the millionth time—I wondered if having one leg simply made me too flawed to carry on a normal life. But carry on I did, to the best of my ability.

The reason I'd gone back to school in the first place was that, during my three-year hiatus from college, and through my experiences connecting with other disabled folks, I'd discovered the healing power of recreation. And so, I'd returned to college to earn a degree in Therapeutic Recreation. And it was through my educational pursuits up in Bellingham that I met Eric.

My second year back at school, I enrolled in an experiential outdoor education program that focused on nature-based learning. With fifteen other students, I went rock climbing, created an educational nature curriculum for fifth graders, and taught the fifth graders about different habitats during a weeklong immersion camp. I snow-camped on Mt. Baker, and took a two-week backpacking trip in the Pasayten Wilderness, three days of which were a solo experience for each of us. All of this was exciting and gratifying.

And hovering in the background of my adventures was Eric, one of my classmates and a regular among those I hung out with. He was the mountain man of the group. He was six foot five and skinny as a rail, with a rugged face and a scruff of auburn hair. His smile was quick and huge, revealing big white teeth. He was only twenty-five, but the wrinkles around his eyes were those of a man who had spent years living outdoors, squinting into the sun. Eric was a hunter, fisherman, and nature lover. On our backpacking trip into the Pasayten, he not only identified every birdcall, but also imitated each call to near perfection. And then he would inform us of the bird's mating habits and migratory patterns. Always good for a laugh, Eric would recount these facts in a British accent while rubbing his chin with exaggerated thoughtfulness. He made me laugh with all his accents and crude remarks, though he often also made me cringe with his thoughtlessly rude comments. I didn't want to admit to myself that I was attracted to Eric, but I caught myself watching him out of the corner of my eye.

The end of the quarter marked the beginning of summer. Most everyone had left town, but I attempted to have an end-of-the-year potluck for the few stragglers of the group who'd remained. In a funny—if not awkward—twist, my timing was off, and the only person who ended up coming was Eric. After a half hour of drinking beer and waiting for the others to show up, we realized we would be eating alone. Eric and I had never spent time alone together, and my hidden infatuation was poking out its timid head.

"Well, Red, looks like it's just you and me eatin' this grub," he said in his cowboy accent. He took a puff of his hand-rolled cigarette, squinting to avoid the smoke. My heart dropped to my knees. I was speechless, but I giggled.

After dinner, we decided to take a walk on a nearby beach. I learned more about him and his upbringing, and he finally broke the privacy barrier and asked how I'd lost my leg.

"When I first saw you walking into the classroom, I thought it was such a shame that a pretty young thing like you was limping," he said, which was the kind of thoughtless, rude comment that made me want to slap him. And yet it was honest enough that I also appreciated it.

"What!" I screamed, and I slapped him on the shoulder with a smile.

He laughed. "I'm sorry, I just think it's too bad this happened to someone as lovely as you, my dear." The kind, elderly British gentleman was back.

"Well, I'm learning a lot from this," I said, trying to remain philosophical for the sake of our conversation. "Being an amputee has taught me a lot about myself and about other people." This was true, of course, though not the whole story.

Eric squinted into the setting sun, and I could see him take in my comment. I let the silence linger. He had his own brand of uniqueness, and whether he knew it or not, I thought he could relate to what I was talking about. I found that to be true for a lot of people. They admired me for how I'd handled my situation, forgetting to admire themselves for how they had managed their own hardships. I was far enough into my journey to know that suffering touched everyone in one way or another.

That evening didn't end. We went back to my house and spent the rest of the night exploring each other in completely new ways.

Two days later, Eric left to go fishing in Alaska for the summer. I was confused about how to say good-bye. Did we have a one-night fling? Did we just cement our relationship? Eric was another solo traveler, like Rob, so I decided on a casual good-bye. He followed suit. "Of all the gin joints in all the world, I had to find you in this one," he said in his Humphrey Bogart accent. He gave me a big hug punctuated by a low dip in his strong right arm. "I'll be seeing you, in all the old familiar places," he crooned, and then he headed out the door.

What did that mean? What the hell did I just do? I didn't know where to put this relationship or how to categorize it. Clearly he wasn't my boyfriend, and the concept of "friends with benefits" had only recently been introduced to me. I didn't think I wanted that. But he was gone for the summer, and I was left working at my internship, confused and hopeful for fall.

In early September, I received a phone call.

"Hello?"

"Yes, hello," said the deep voice of what sounded like a radio pitchman. "Is this Red? Because if it is, have I got a deal for you. You've just been awarded a dinner out to Bellingham's finest restaurant." My face flushed as I realized it was Eric.

"Hi, Eric," I managed to blurt out, feeling suddenly self-conscious. "How was fishing?"

"Ah, hell," he said in his grumbly cowboy voice. "You know, ya win some, ya lose some. But I did make enough to take a purty young lady to dinner. Waddaya say, Missy?" He ended his speech in a full John Wayne.

"Great! When?"

"How about six?"

"Tonight?"

"Yep, tonight."

I had enough time to bathe, shave my leg, and wash my hair. All the while the butterflies of excitement fluttered in my stomach. I didn't want to admit to myself all summer how much I was hoping he'd call, and now that he had, I was overjoyed.

When he came to the door, Eric greeted me with a long, slow kiss. I just about melted to the floor. "Good to see you, Red," he said softly in my ear in his own voice.

"Good to see you, too," I whispered back.

Eric was good for me. He made sure I kept hiking, even though school was now back in the classroom. We took beautiful fall walks on old logging roads. He took me target shooting, and I even tried my hand at grouse hunting. I didn't like the guns, but I loved hearing his endless knowledge of nature: birds, animals, plants, trees. I was a sponge, and he was a flowing river of information.

The first week of December, I realized my period was late. My dread mounted every time I went to the bathroom and searched for the blood spot on my underwear that should have been there by now. One evening, as I was in the bathroom and Eric was in the living room, I became light-headed. The sound of rushing blood filled my ears. Though my eyes were open, my world turned black. I was being lifted out of my body and up into the cosmos. All I could see were stars, millions and millions of stars. I crumpled to the bathroom floor. I heard Eric's feet taking one, two, only three steps from the living room to the bathroom.

"What the . . . ?" Arms enveloped me. My head was too heavy to hold up, so I rested it against his chest. My eyelids were too heavy to keep open, so I closed them. A rush of warmth circled my face, and I felt the distantly familiar need to throw up. Right now. I heaved myself off of Eric's chest and threw myself over the tub, letting it all out, not even embarrassed that Eric was right there.

"Hey, you all right? What's going on?" he said, his voice his own but concerned.

"Oh, Eric, I think I'm pregnant." The knot of guilt was back in my stomach. Tears filled my eyes. Cold pressure filled my chest as I realized what was happening to my body again.

"Well, shit."

I didn't expect Eric to be happy, but that wasn't the support I was looking for.

"Well, before you get all freaked out, let's find out for sure," I said, miffed. I still didn't want to admit it. I just wanted a nice evening making dinner, but Eric needed to know. He made sure I was tucked into bed and then went to the store to buy a home pregnancy test.

Eric was still sleeping when I took the test the next morning. A big plus sign was staring me in the face.

How could I have let this happen again? How could I be so stupid?

I had been using my diaphragm, but not religiously. My negligence was coming back to haunt me. I was filled with dread. Dread for the immediacy of needing to make a decision. Dread for my future if I made the decision to keep the baby. Dread when I thought about telling my family. I went back to bed, lay next to Eric, and sobbed in his arms, wishing he knew how to take care of this. Eric could build an ice cave, tie any kind of knot, and shoot a deer with a bow and arrow, but he was at a loss when confronted with this.

"Colleen, you know I don't want to have kids. Hell, woman, I don't even want to get married. You know that. The decision is yours, and I'll support you financially if you decide to keep the kid, but I can't be a dad."

If there was one thing I appreciated about Eric, it was his honesty. I don't think he even knew how to lie. That, mixed with his lack of tact, made him say a lot of insensitive things, but I appreciated hearing the God's honest truth. If I was going to have this baby, I would be a single mother with a child-support check coming in the mail every month. What had my life become? Was I really going to end up a single mother at twenty-six years old?

As I lay in bed ruminating, what really nagged at me was my body. I felt like I was at the top of my game—as healthy and strong as I'd ever been or was likely to ever be. I was a skier, a backpacker, and an explorer of many other sports and activities. I knew my body was capable of doing so many adventurous things, but I wasn't convinced I could maintain my mobility if I went through a pregnancy.

However, my most prevalent thought was that I should have made sure not to let myself get into this situation again. I already carried too much guilt from the first pregnancy to have another abortion. I should have been more responsible. I should have been more careful. I should have known better. Now I had to deal with the consequences.

I thought back to my visit at Kevin and Molly's house after Brendon was born. Holding him was unlike anything I'd experienced. I had seen the grandeur of a mountaintop, felt the exhilaration of skiing down a fast slope, and heard the melancholy cry of the bald eagle, but I had never felt such fragile, vulnerable strength in my life. How could I abort another baby now that I knew how precious babies were? He was so tiny and so perfect. I thought of the agony I felt holding Brendon; he represented the loss of my own baby. Could I expose myself to another loss?

But I was not a fully formed adult yet myself. No one who carries a milestone of shame and guilt around their neck can reach her highest potential. A year prior, Father Dempsey had told me my abortion was unforgiveable. I was still conflicted and angry about that. I had a hard time accepting I was unforgiveable, but I was having an equally hard time believing a priest could be so wrong. And I certainly did not feel forgiven. I hadn't forgiven myself, after all.

That night was my friend Sandra's rehearsal dinner; she was getting married the next day, and I was the maid of honor. I'd met Sandra in the Therapeutic Recreation program, and had been excited when she asked me to be in her wedding. I went to the dinner without Eric, feeling numb and shell-shocked. I did the best I could at the event, but watching her look at the man she loved with an intimate smile, knowing they were promising to be together forever and have children together, made me so sad for myself. I desperately wanted the life she was stepping into, what Mom and Dad had had. I wanted to find a soul mate, the love of my life—and have babies once the love was in place.

The next day I got ready for the wedding, and Eric helped me prepare for the party I was throwing at my house after the reception. I wanted to stay present for Sandra—girlfriends for me were hard to come by, and I intended to do right by those friendships I'd developed in Bellingham. I knew from my first pregnancy that I had a week or two to figure this out. So I pretended I wasn't pregnant and tucked my feelings aside for the day. At the party at my house after the reception, I got good and drunk and acted like I didn't have a care in the world. But the knot of guilt grew bigger, even more so now that I was drinking with a baby inside me.

My sister-in-law Molly was newly pregnant with Brendon's

sibling. How could I say no while Molly was saying yes? Even if I still couldn't imagine myself as a mother, I could do the admirable thing and give the baby up for adoption.

"Eric, I don't think I can go through another abortion." We had talked about my previous abortion over the past week. "The last one was so hard; I still don't think I'm over it. So I've decided to give the baby up for adoption."

"Ah, geez, really? Have you thought about this? I mean, if I don't have to be responsible for a little kid for the rest of my life, I would be so grateful, but I know your family is really important to you. Do you really think you can give the baby up?"

"Hell, I've done a lot of hard things in my life. I'd rather give the baby up than not give it a chance at life. I think I need to do the responsible thing and at least bring this baby into the world."

"But I'm not convinced you won't be torn up about it later on. You're strong, but you're not that strong." He was just trying to convince me to abort the baby, which pissed me off.

"Unless you're going to be the father of this baby, you don't really have any say in the matter. I'll do what I want. And right now I just want to go to bed."

"Well, all right then, but don't come crying to me every year on the kid's birthday."

"You can be sure I won't."

Eric had been clear from the get-go that he wasn't the marrying kind. I didn't mind; I didn't want to marry him anyway. He drank too much, and he was crude and too rude for my taste, but I couldn't help but love him. We'd made our relationship exclusive, but we knew it was temporary.

Finals were the next week, so I focused my attention on them. I was a much better student after my three-year break from school, and I wanted to ace my tests. I'd found out about this pregnancy four weeks earlier than the last one and wasn't suffering from constant nausea like before, but I had an incessant pounding headache.

I did well on my tests. And once I had some breathing room in my schedule, I had time to think things through more clearly. I realized I hadn't put all the pieces of my life together. If I was going to carry this baby to term, I'd be pregnant during my upcoming internship. After which, I'd still have two quarters of college left. Would I ever finish school if I was pregnant for the next nine months? In the quiet of my post-finals life, my commitment to see the pregnancy through began to wane.

In a fit of panic and loneliness, I visited my friend Luann, one of the outdoor crew I'd grown close to while backpacking earlier in the academic year. I was embarrassed to admit I was in this predicament, but I needed to talk to someone and get some advice. I practically ran into her arms when I saw her, so desperate was I for a hug. I felt so distressed that I started sobbing.

"What is it, Colleen? What's wrong?" Luann seemed to have a charmed life, and her voice was light and casual.

"The worst thing ever," I sobbed onto her shoulder. *Boy, she doesn't see this coming.*

"Your mom died?" She pulled me away by the shoulders and looked at me in concern. *Oh my god*, I thought, *she's right.* It was good perspective to remember that something like my mom dying would be much worse than this.

"No, I'm *pregnant.*" Not death, but new life.

With a little laugh, she said, "Oh, is that all?"

I shook my head in disbelief and sat down at the kitchen table. "Luann, this is a big deal. I'm thinking of giving the baby up for adoption."

"Oh." She sat down with me. "Well, if that's what you want." Her brow furrowed. "Why don't you just have an abortion?" I loved Luann. I respected her and her liberal, freestyle thinking. But even this was a little cavalier for me.

"Luann, abortion is a sin." I heard a plea in my voice as if trying to convince her.

"Oh, you still believe that?" She looked at me wide-eyed. I didn't want to believe in predetermined sin, but Catholic dogma was ingrained in me. I tried to look at my choices outside of that construct, but Father Dempsey's judgment was like a claw in my back.

Luann had grown up in an Italian Catholic family, so she knew what I was faced with. I admired how she had given up the Catholic faith so easily, with no looking back. Me? I'd given lip service to letting go of Catholicism when among my liberal friends, but I kept looking over my shoulder, watching it follow me, feeling it lurk behind every decision I made.

"I do believe it," I said.

Luann reached out and put her hands on mine. "Colleen, whose life is this? It's yours, isn't it? And who else knows the big picture of everything you're dealing with?"

"No one," I replied, dabbing at my tears.

"Well, if *you* can't trust *you* to make a decision for *you*, I don't know who else you're going to trust the rest of your life."

Why those simple words hit me so hard, I don't really know. But what I did know was that she was right. It was time I figured out how to be responsible for my choices, and to think through my options based on what made sense for me rather than on who would judge me. Even God couldn't live my life for me. It was all on me.

I got up, dried my face with my sleeve, and hugged Luann good-bye.

Luann didn't tell me what to do. In fact, she did something even more powerful. She convinced me I could make the right decision for myself.

That night I went to bed alone, puzzling about what to do. I woke up the next morning with a start. My eyes snapped open, and I heard the words: "You can't have this baby." I looked around, scared, but no one else was in my room. My heart was racing as I lay my head back down on my pillow. And then I remembered a dream I'd had the night before: I was eight months pregnant and in the grocery store. I was so big I was unrecognizable to myself. I couldn't fit into my prosthetic leg anymore, so I was using crutches. My pregnant belly stuck out so far, I couldn't reach the handle of the grocery cart. I was looking around for someone to help me, but everyone was ignoring the huge, one-legged pregnant lady. I started screaming for help, but no one would help me. I was all alone and completely incapable of taking care of myself.

I got out of bed and knew what I had to do. I walked to the phone, looked up a clinic, and made the call.

"Yes, I'd like to make an appointment to terminate my pregnancy."

Eric drove me to the appointment and waited in the lobby. I had to do this one alone since it was my decision. The procedure hadn't changed: Undress, put on the gown, stick my feet in the stirrups, and do what the mechanical voice of the doctor said. Whisper "I'm sorry" over and over while this precious new life is being sucked into oblivion. "I'm so sorry. I'm so sorry. Please come back to me when I'm ready. I'm not saying I don't want you; I just don't want you right now. I'm so sorry." Allow the tears to flow. Feel the gentle pat of the nurse's hand on my shoulder. Try to listen to the post-procedure instructions . . . but hear only the blood rushing through my head. Nod in understanding, even though I really don't understand.

I was left alone in the exam room to get dressed. My hands were shaking so much I could barely adhere the Kotex pad to my underwear to catch the leftover blood. My legs could hardly hold me up. I slowly walked out into the lobby, using the wall to steady myself, and I spotted Eric. When he saw me, he put down the *Field & Stream* magazine and quickly walked up to me.

"How ya doing, Red?"

"Not so good. Just get me home."

He held me up by taking my arm and guided me to the car and gently put me in it.

"Well, that didn't take long."

Yeah, it's amazing how quickly one can snuff out a life.

"Shut up," I said. "Just shut the fuck up. I don't want to hear any kind of relief in your voice right now. I just did the hardest thing in my life, and I need you to just shut up. When we get home, I need you to lie down next to me, hold me, and let me cry until I'm done. Okay? Can you do that?" I asked, ending with a plea.

"Yeah. I can do that."

I cried quietly all the way home. I cried silently as he walked me into the house. I cried as he took off my jacket and shoes and tucked me into bed. I cried as he spooned me, holding me tight. The pain was so deep, the reality of what I'd done so raw, all I could do was groan through the tears. And then I heard him let out a little cry, too, which made me feel a tiny bit better.

I cried until I finally fell asleep. When I woke up, the early winter darkness had descended, mirroring the darkness in my heart. During my sleep, I could tell my layer of armor had thickened once again. My sadness was too huge to let out; I had to contain it. I smelled the stir-fry Eric was cooking. I tried to eat, but the food tasted like cardboard. Eric looked at me, uncharacteristically serious. He took my hand, and said very quietly, "Thank you." I wanted to slap him again. I wanted to shove him down a flight of stairs. I hated his gratefulness for what I'd done. I hated that I was probably just as relieved as he was. He just had the balls to own up to it. And even though I'd been the one to make this decision for myself, it wasn't any easier this time through. I was as embroiled in guilt and remorse as ever.

I knew I had to do something before my insides rotted away with the ugliness I carried there.

13
• ● •
BABY BUNDLES

Eric and I broke up when I went to Minnesota for my internship a month after the abortion. I finished college the following year. The summer after graduation, I took a month-long sea-kayaking course taught by the National Outdoor Leadership School in Alaska. I had been toying with the idea of starting my own therapeutic recreation business and I wanted to see firsthand how I fared as a leader in that environment. In all my outdoor pursuits thus far I had felt confident, but I always needed help in one way or another because of my leg. Could I be a leader and help others without needing help myself? Unfortunately, halfway through the kayak trip, my peg leg broke and my guide had to help me jerry-rig it back together. Perhaps I sold myself short, perhaps I gave up too early, but that experience, for as awe-inspiring as it was to kayak in Alaska for a month, solidified the notion that I didn't have what it took to be an outdoor leader.

After that summer, I started my career working as camp director at a summer camp for people with developmental disabilities in Idaho. I no longer felt stigmatized to be associated with developmentally disabled folks like I had on the Skiforall bus so many years ago. In fact, I felt honored to be able to provide a place for them to feel included, something I had been searching for since my accident. Though I'd struggled to find connections in my own life, it turned out I was good at creating them for others who sought them out.

Over the years, all but one of my siblings had gotten married and started families. A new niece or nephew came along every year or two. Each time I visited a new baby, my grief was reignited. Each time, I swallowed the lump of regret in my throat. Each time, I reminded myself I made the choice to have an abortion so that I could live my life, my active life. I continued to ski in the winter and backpack and kayak in the summer.

After two summers at camp, I moved back to Seattle to work with adults with developmental disabilities, supporting them to live independently. Suppressing my grief—for the loss of my leg and my two abortions—was second nature to me by then. I continued to search for activities that brought joy and meaning to my life. I joined a dojo that taught Aikido, a martial art that focused on nonresistance. This practice nurtured my spiritual cravings as well as my physical ones. My sensei, or teacher, accommodated my needs well; I learned how to fall and roll alongside the other students. I went to class twice a week. With each move the sensei taught, she tied it to one of the principles of Aikido: see things from another's perspective, help others see things from your perspective, and strive for harmony.

The summer of my thirty-first year, my suppressed grief was catching up with me. Driving to work became increasingly difficult. When a car started merging into my lane, I panicked. All I could see was that white bread truck from fourteen years ago merging into our lane. I played out the scenario of my accident over and over. And I created new scenarios in my mind of getting hit present day. I sobbed as I relived the memories and thought about the possibility of getting hurt again. There were instances when I was so scared or I was crying so hard that I had to pull over and collect myself. Friends asked me to go with them to a Bonnie Raitt concert that was a four-hour drive away and I said no, not because I didn't want to go—I did—but because I knew I couldn't be in a car on the freeway for that long. I'd be a crumpled mess by the time we arrived.

No one really knows why trauma symptoms emerge or worsen many years after the inciting incident, but emerge they did for me. At the dojo on a sunny Sunday morning, we were practicing a new move. The sensei talked about compassion and patience, nonresistance and harmony. My partner threw me to the mat in a way I had been thrown many times during the previous year. But that time when I landed on my back, I suddenly felt like I was back on the highway, lying next to our car, waiting for the ambulance to arrive. Everything I was resisting in my emotional life came crashing down on me. I gasped and felt as if I was falling into a black hole. I slapped my hands on the mat to bring me back into the room. I had stuffed my sadness this many years; I wasn't about to let my grief spill out here on the dojo mat, but internally I was a mess. I got up, scrambled over to the shoes, grabbed mine, and left the dojo as fast as my legs could carry me. I started sobbing, just as I had when I left Father Dempsey's office, trying desperately to keep myself together. What happened that Sunday at the dojo was terrifying, and I wasn't willing to let that happen again. So I never went back.

Though I couldn't put these words to it then, my world was becoming small. I started living with fear—of getting hit by another car, of my grief, of my future that was looking more and more like I was going to be on my own.

I knew my emotions were bottled up and unresolved, but that was the only way I knew how to be. I didn't know *how* to grieve. Instead of going back to the dojo, I went to see a therapist, Lynn. When I first met her, I told her that I was there to "get over my accident" and I wanted to wrap this up in six months. Lynn suppressed a laugh and told me it might take a little longer than that.

I didn't know a lot about post-traumatic stress disorder, but Lynn did. She created a nurturing, warm environment. Sitting in her office was like being in a cocoon of comfort. During one of our first visits, I was explaining to her how the accident happened. I had learned to talk about this moment of my life with the practiced authority of an orator. I spoke with little emotion, a master at hiding my feelings. As I was explaining why it took so long for the ambulance to arrive on the scene of the accident, a siren started wailing outside Lynn's window. My voice cracked, but I continued my narrative. Lynn gently asked me to stop talking.

"Listen to that siren, Colleen." The siren howled louder. "How does that make you feel?" Ever since the accident, the sound of an ambulance sent my heart racing, which made me feel foolish and weak, not strong like I had convinced myself I needed to be. Sitting there with Lynn, in that warm room, I allowed myself to give in to the anguish. I couldn't respond to her. I could only sob.

Lynn told me about the Wailing Wall in Jerusalem and explained that people go there to grieve. On purpose. There is no shame in the tears that fall at the Wailing Wall. There is no expectation to be stoic. I was aware that though I had cried a lot over the years, I had stifled my deepest grief, but Lynn's permission to express it was the first time I felt safe doing so. She loaned me a piece of the Wailing Wall, about the size of a small stone, which someone had brought her from Jerusalem. I tucked it into a leather pouch and wore it around my neck every day for months. Here was a construct for healing that was far removed from my Catholic upbringing—no shame required. I rubbed the rock whenever I heard sirens, whenever my leg hurt, whenever I felt sad. I learned how to allow the sadness to bubble to the surface instead of constantly shoving it down.

Lynn likened the process of grieving to that of peeling an onion. When I peeled an onion later at home, the first papery layer was hard to remove because it was clinging to the onion. After I peeled it off, I noticed how transparent it was. I wondered if the emotions sitting on the surface of my heart were going to be equally difficult to peel away. I wondered if they were just a mirror of what lay beneath. Lynn worked with me on how to appropriately express emotions, how to ask for help, how to be vulnerable.

As I grieved for my accident, I also allowed myself to process my feelings about my abortions. Lynn asked if doing a ritual would bring closure to those experiences. I liked that idea. On a Saturday morning I made two small figures, each about two inches long. I took scraps of fabric and made crude bundles resembling swaddled babies, one purple and one green. With colorful beads from my craft cupboard, I decorated the bundles by sewing spirals and stars on the fabric. Intuitively I knew one was a boy and one was a girl. I carried the baby bundles around delicately in my pockets for four days—four representing the four seasons of the year, the seasons they did not live through because of my decision to terminate their lives. On the fourth day I then took them to an old-growth park near my home and buried them under the largest cedar tree I could find. The cedar felt protective and wise. I wanted to give my little beings a proper burial. With my bare hands, I dug a shallow grave in the soft ground under the cedar and set the two bundles inside, resting them side by side. I sang a Native American chant I had learned from a medicine woman I'd studied with a few years earlier. After I covered the bundles with the earth, I sat down and leaned against the tree and meditated. I envisioned these two little souls soaring into the heavens, free and happy.

The process of burying these bundles helped me exhume my grief. I felt lighter after the ritual, having brought closure, as much as I could at that point, to the decisions I made. When I buried those bundles, I made the decision to let go of the regret and self-recrimination that I had held on to for so many years. I forgave the unforgivable.

14
• ● •
FORGIVING THE UNFORGIVABLE

Every year in early January I fell into the depths of contemplation and depression as I neared the anniversary of the accident. It was on the fifteenth anniversary, when I was thirty-two years old, that something snapped as I sat in my living room waiting for a phone call I didn't know I was waiting for. Like an unexpected punch to the gut, I realized that Harvey had never contacted me to be sure I was okay.

After the trial, he never wrote a nice note of apology for ruining my life. He never drove down to see me to make sure that I was real and not the recurring nightmare I hoped I was to him at night. I was suddenly consumed with a rage, pure and direct.

I decided to call him. Right then. I'd show him what a nightmare was like. There was no stopping me.

As the dark outside turned darker on January 3, 1993, I got off my sofa and walked decidedly to the phone sitting on my desk. I called directory assistance to get his number in Victoria, BC, where I knew he lived. They only had his mother's number, so I called her. Simple as that. I didn't know if she was aware that her son had ripped away a young women's leg, so I just left my name and number and asked her to have him contact me. I went to bed feeling relieved that I had finally figured out where to target my anger.

At work the next day, I wondered: Will he call? Does he remember my name? Does he even know what yesterday was? I was afraid

I would have to embarrass myself by explaining what he'd done to me before I yelled at him for having done it. Would he call me, or ignore my message, afraid of what I might say to him? By the time I got home from work, I was a nervous wreck. As I waited for his call, I paced and smoked, smoked and paced. And then the phone rang.

"Hello?"

His slight Canadian accent responded, "Hello Colleen, this is Harvey."

"Do you remember who I am?" I screamed, bracing myself against my desk. The sound of his voice was like a gust of strong wind, threatening to knock me over.

Through his own grave sobs, he responded, "Oh, yes."

"Do you know what yesterday was?" I demanded, surprised that he was emotional, too, but not willing to give up my rehearsed series of questions.

"Oh, yes," he cried. "I think of you every year. I think of you all the time."

What was he doing, crying like that? How could I be angry at him now? How could I make my case? Soon he was saying, "I'm sorry," over and over again on the other end of the line. This wasn't going the way I wanted. His willingness to apologize got me off track. I wasn't sure which way to go.

We ended the call when Harvey offered to meet with me. I put the receiver back in its cradle and sat down on the floor near the phone, my breathing shallow. What had just happened?

Meeting with the man who had changed the direction of my life felt risky and bold, but I decided I had to do it. I had waited a very long time to face this down—to face him down. We agreed to meet in Victoria. He still hadn't traveled south on the road on which the accident had happened. He said that coming to Seattle would be too difficult for him—could I come to Canada?

Too difficult?

Because I'd gone to college near the accident site, I had traveled that road countless times. Each time I drove past the place where

I'd lost my leg, the metallic taste of shock saturated my mouth. Sometimes I cried. Sometimes I continued my conversation with the person I was driving with, and pretended it was just any other piece of roadway. Sometimes I hid my feelings by lighting up another cigarette. Too difficult? He didn't know what difficult was. But, true to character, I decided to take care of his needs more than my own and drive up to see him.

In preparation for our meeting, I spent five sessions with Lynn, preparing my list of all the reasons I was so angry. My anger at what happened had never been this consciously directed before. It was a relief to finally target my anger where it belonged: at Harvey.

My brother Matthew and his boyfriend, Kirk, accompanied me to Victoria. We stayed at the Empress Hotel on Valentine's weekend. The irony that I would be meeting Harvey on Valentine's Day didn't miss me. Love is a bond that inextricably connects two hearts. Harvey and I were connected—no question about that. And so we were to experience a unique kind of love that Valentine's Day.

We agreed to meet in the lobby of the hotel. At the appointed time, Matthew and Kirk walked with me, steadying me as we descended the ramp into the lobby.

"Do you want us to stay until you find him?" Matthew asked.

"No, I need to do this alone," I replied. They both gave me hugs and slowly walked back up the ramp, glancing over their shoulders as they walked. I peered over mine for one last encouraging glance.

I felt as fierce as a lioness protecting her cub—and as vulnerable as the cub itself. I imagined seeing Harvey and running up to him, even though I can't run, and hitting him repeatedly in the chest, screaming every profanity I could imagine. This fantasy of hitting and hitting and hitting him was very consoling. I couldn't wait.

Armored by my anger, shaking from my fear, I searched the lobby for a face I didn't really remember. A sea of people checking in for the weekend congested the room. I started feeling lightheaded as I scanned the crowd. Then I saw him: a big lug of a man, walking toward me. Oh, no. I had forgotten how big he was. *He's too big to hit*, I thought.

As he got closer, I could see he was crying. *Wait: I'm the one who should be crying*, I thought. *Aren't I?* I had it planned out in my head that I was going to yell and scream at him, hit him, and rub in his face how much the accident had impacted my life. I planned to shower shame on him, to take the mantle of pain off my shoulders and place it squarely on his where it belonged. His tears and my early training in empathy toward those who were suffering were going to make that very difficult. He walked right up to me and asked me for a hug. I didn't want to hug him, but I didn't know how to say no, so I hugged him.

We decided to take a walk in the hotel gardens. Even when I put a lot of effort into walking correctly, I still limp. That day, as we strolled around the gardens, I did my best walking. I certainly didn't accentuate my limp. But I was secretly glad that he could finally see me move, impaired by what he'd done to me.

After a while we went into the bar and drank beer and smoked cigarettes—like any two people might do. He began to talk. And my resolve, my need to hurt him as he'd hurt me, dissolved with the outpouring of words I hadn't known I needed to hear.

"I've always thought about you . . . When I see a young woman who looks like you, my day is ruined . . . My life was devastated because of this."

Harvey and I talked about how the accident had altered his life. Anytime the reality of what happened hit him, anytime he saw a woman who looked like me, he became moody and mean. "I became like Dr. Jekyll and Mr. Hyde: nice guy one minute and angry the next," he sobbed. I could see the pain and guilt in his tear-filled eyes. "My wife couldn't take it anymore. She finally divorced me." He wiped away a tear. "I replay the accident over and over and try to see what I could have done differently," he explained. His face contorted in anguish, expressing exactly what I felt inside but didn't have the heart to say.

I didn't expect this. I had thought this was going to be my show. But now, I couldn't spill my guts and slap him with the reality of how altered my own life had become. How I question my attractiveness as a woman because I limp around on a plastic leg. How I have to mentally prepare myself for a simple walk around the neighborhood with my dog. How I feel distant from others because they don't understand my pain. I couldn't paint for him the picture of how my amputation had affected my daily life. The obvious pain his guilt was causing him proved to me that he had been through enough.

"I'd give you my leg if I could," he offered.

"I don't want your leg, Harvey," I told him. I just needed to see his remorse. And I clearly had that.

Harvey told me that when he went to counseling, his therapist pushed the idea that what happened wasn't his fault. It was an accident. This was a change in perspective for me: *It was an accident.* I had always said to myself, "I was in an accident; but it was Harvey's fault." I sat holding my cigarette pondering the possibility that accidents don't have fault. They simply are. Could that be true?

Harvey and I reviewed the accident in detail. Though we had heard it all at the trial thirteen years before, we both needed to review the specific facts now. I'd never really considered that Harvey would have his own perspective.

"Our car had spun out on the snowy freeway. When we came to a stop, we were facing traffic," I explained.

"Why were you out of the car?" he asked.

"No one was stopping to help us. I wanted to flag down some help. All the cars were driving slowly by us in the right lane; I thought for sure someone could help me stop traffic so we could turn the car around and merge back into traffic." I paused. Here I was, retelling the story *again*, but this time to the other main character: Harvey. The moment felt surreal. "Why were you in the left lane going so fast?" I asked.

"I didn't think I was going fast. When I saw you, I tried to get out of the way and merge into the right lane, but the snow buildup between the lanes caused my car to swerve. I lost control of my car and started spinning. That's when I hit you."

My mouth was dry from the beer, the cigarettes, and the emotion. We had said all there was to say. We couldn't dissect it further. Though the resolution I'd hoped for didn't feel perfectly complete, I felt as if I'd done all I could do by coming to Victoria and spending an afternoon with the man whose visage had tormented me all these years. And Harvey had given me this time. He'd done all he could do given his own pain.

He walked me back to the lobby and I hugged him again. But this time I wanted to.

I returned to the hotel room in a fog of emotions. Matthew and Kirk immediately turned off the TV and looked at me with expectant eyes. "It was good," was all I could muster. They stood up and, with their four huge arms, protectively embraced me. I allowed myself to be enfolded in their love. My brain was full, and I could feel the stirrings of a shift in my heart.

When I realized I could see the accident from Harvey's perspective I felt a freedom I hadn't known before. I didn't know it earlier, but now I could see that bitterness only hurts the one who holds it in her body. During my visit with Harvey, I didn't utter the words "I forgive you," but after the visit, I forgave Harvey in my heart. That was one of the most empowering things I have ever done. Nothing on the outside had changed—I still didn't have my leg, it still hurt to walk, and I still got stares from strangers—but so much on the inside was different.

PART II

• ● •

The hardest to learn was the least complicated.

—the Indigo Girls

15

. ● .

TRUE LOVE

was on a journey of healing, and I was grateful to finally have a guide in Lynn. But the road ahead was going to be long, and I wasn't getting any younger—wasn't becoming more eligible or more fertile. After having the men I'd loved tell me how beautiful I was, how wonderful I was, but that they couldn't marry me, I started to consider that maybe my life could be different than the norm in more ways than just the fact that I was missing my leg. Perhaps I wouldn't ever get married like my siblings and friends. And maybe that was okay. Once I'd forgiven myself for the abortions and for-given Harvey for indelibly altering my life, I allowed myself to consider life without a man. And this idea made me feel so free. Perhaps I could live life on my own terms, with a boy-toy thrown in for good measure now and again if that's what I wanted. Perhaps I didn't need a man—or children—to complete my life. Perhaps I could go through life by myself and still be happy.

I started living my life as if I would spend the rest of it on my own. In my early thirties, I took a three-week trip to Mexico and had a great vacation. Alone. I decided I was a great traveling com-panion. To myself. I thought about buying a house. For myself. I looked into joining the Peace Corps. I searched master's programs at local universities. If a husband and family weren't going to fulfill my life, I'd find other passions to bring me joy.

Then something happened that often happens once a person

starts forgiving her past and genuinely lets go of her dreams. They started to come true.

I met Mark.

I was Mark's supervisor at a social services agency in Seattle for a year and a half before we connected romantically. I found myself looking at him, especially as he walked away, to catch a glimpse of his cute butt. I chatted too long at his workstation and was surprised at myself, both that I was flirting and that I was enjoying it without any sense of urgency or self-recrimination. Mark had been flirting with me, too, but he was proper and appropriate in the workplace. He was a part of a small group of us who occasionally went out together for drinks. The group had even been to my apartment a few times. When he told me he was applying to the Peace Corps and might be leaving in the months to come, I decided to throw caution to the wind. What the hell. I was in charge of my life now. If he was leaving, I had nothing to lose; we could have a little fun before he left.

I invited Mark over to my place for breakfast. He came over on a hot August Sunday morning. I tried to pretend I was cool as a cucumber, but when I found myself on the phone with my brother David an hour before Mark arrived, frantically asking how to make a Greek omelet, my stomach tied up in knots, I knew I was in trouble. It was Mark who appeared casual and at ease during breakfast and even during our walk on Alki Beach, just a block from my apartment. As we sat on a log watching the Bremerton ferry slide across the sun-sparkled water, I watched his green eyes track a seagull through the air and his curly hair blow slightly in the wind. Then I just blurted it out: I was attracted to him.

That was all we needed. Someone had to break the ice. We walked back across the beach, hand in hand. That was enough. That was everything.

A month later, Mark and I took a camping trip to the coast for the weekend. I wore my peg leg. I knew I'd come a long way when I didn't fear his attraction to me would dissipate at the sight of my crude water leg. Our hike was a three-mile trip on a boardwalk through a moss-laden forest. The boardwalk was covered in a thin layer of slime, making it quite slick. I suddenly found myself on my butt, my backpack laying catawampus by my side. Mark and I were equally surprised by my fall. I, the seasoned backpacker, was initially embarrassed, but then I accepted, again and sincerely, this was just who I was. Self-acceptance is a gentle but powerful feeling. I sat for a moment and collected myself.

Mark quietly took my hand, and for the rest of the hike, we walked slowly over the boardwalk. I was hunched over like an old woman taking baby steps to avoid falling again, loving every minute with him. Had I really grown and changed so much that I could fall on my ass in front of someone I was attracted to and still enjoy myself? Or was Mark an incredibly special man? Maybe it was both.

Regardless, I felt solid in who I was, both as a woman and as an amputee. Take me or leave me, I was finally in a space where I didn't care more about what other people thought than about being myself. Mark and I talked and talked, and I fell in love with him on our hike. Truly in love. His kindness was quiet and powerful. He didn't use words to prove his acceptance of me; his actions said it all.

Together we talked to my administrator and requested Mark's supervision be transferred to my peer. After three more months, he withdrew his candidacy for the Peace Corps.

In February, we took a weekend getaway to Orcas Island. Over dinner, we got engaged. I felt as giddy as a little girl in Disneyland and as grounded as the cedar trees outside the windows. The next morning, as we stood on the grassy cliffs, overlooking the San Juan Islands, sailboats gliding across the water like whales, I broached the subject that was always at the forefront of my mind.

"Mark, my leg will matter. If we get married, I don't know how it will affect our lives in the long run. When I'm an old lady, walking may be hard for me."

"I know." Quietly. Sincerely.

"But I really don't know what I will be like. What if I can't walk?"

"We'll be fine." Did I hear assurance in his tone, or did I just want to? He didn't seem fazed by how my leg could affect his life. With Mark, I felt whole.

Mark and I wanted our wedding and marriage to be different than the norm. We weren't going to follow the traditional course of middle-class America: have a church wedding, buy a house in the suburbs, have two kids, and join the PTA. Nope. Not for us. Mark and I wanted to do it our way. We talked about taking our kids traveling, exposing them to the world, and living in a culturally diverse neighborhood. Yes, we did talk about children. For me, the topic brought up the tiniest tendrils of worry, since I didn't know what my body was or wasn't capable of, but the guilt I'd lived with for so many years was absent. Gloriously absent.

We had an untraditionally traditional wedding. My brother Matthew signed up to be a legal minister by calling a number from an ad we saw on the back of a matchbook cover. He married us in a beautiful garden. Since I didn't have Dad to walk me down the grass-laden aisle, Mark and I decided to walk together into the circle of a hundred and fifty of our closest family and friends. Standing at the altar, lighting the marriage candle with my groom, who looked so handsome in a double-breasted suit that matched his green eyes, my heart flooded with the warmth of joy and gratitude. I was in awe of this man who was willingly sharing his life with me, and in awe of our deep love. We had written our own vows. When we recited those vows, Mark, a soft-spoken man, read his so loudly he bordered on shouting. Shouting his love for me in front of everyone. My heart nearly burst. Ours was a perfect wedding. We felt held, loved, and supported by everyone there.

16

MY TURN

Mark and I had been married just six months when I became pregnant, nine years after my second abortion. When I saw the plus sign slowly emerge on the pink pregnancy test strip, I was just as shocked as I had been the first two times. The circumstances were playing out once again. Mark and I had been using birth control, but not religiously; we'd assumed safety based on my cycle one too many times. The risk of getting pregnant barely registered. We were married, happy. Secure. Perhaps my sense of security itself loosened my caution.

I should have been happy to see a plus sign, but I wasn't, immediately. I wasn't quite ready for this. *We* weren't ready for this. I felt like our wedding had just been yesterday. We both wanted a child in the abstract, but I especially wanted a longer honeymoon phase before a baby came along. We were just settling in to a routine in a tiny one-bedroom duplex. There was no room for a baby there.

I put down the strip and walked out to the living room. Mark was sitting on the couch, nervously shaking his leg. He looked at me, his eyebrows raised. "Well?" Tears flooded my eyes, and I nodded my head. He rushed over to me and held me tight. "It'll be okay. We'll be fine." But the tightness in his voice gave his feelings away. The fear in my heart was echoed in his tone. I hugged him back. Tightly. We held on to each other for dear life.

Though therapy was helping me heal my guilt and anger, it was also making me very aware of the many fears I carried around about how well I could care for another human being. It had taken me so very long to learn to care for myself with any kind of equanimity. As Mark and I stood embracing, a new level of anxiety began to cluster in my belly. I was no longer a college student afraid of what her mother would think. Instead, I was a grown woman who had worked tirelessly to create a life she could love and respect. Would a child change all of that for me? Would I lose what I had gained by becoming a mother? And what would happen to this body of mine?

"What are we going to do?" I asked.

He grabbed me by the shoulders, gently pushed me away from him, and looked me in the eye, confusion furrowing his brow. "What do you mean?"

"Can we do this?" I said, scared and worried. Did Mark share my fears? Or was I revealing myself as a coward to him?

"I don't know." His brow softened. Did I see relief in his face at my faint suggestion that there was some other choice than having the baby? Then he stroked my hair and said, "Honey, we'll be okay. No matter what, all right?"

"All right. I love you."

"I love you, too," he said, giving me a squeeze.

During my drive to work that morning, I avoided having a cigarette. If ever I needed one it was then. I smoked about eight cigarettes a day, always rationalizing that I deserved each one. They'd been my go-to gals when I was stressed since I'd announced to Rob that I planned to start smoking so many years ago. I felt myself shaking slightly, and my forehead was damp. I knew these telltale physical signs of fear all too well. My therapist had been helping me recognize when post-traumatic stress symptoms were present, and had been walking me through healthier ways of managing them. But right now, all I wanted was a cigarette. I told myself to wait until I arrived at work to have a smoke. The day before, a coworker, Cherie, who knew of my fondness for the color green, gave me two green cigarettes. I could tell how tickled she was to have found them. She could see how delighted I was to receive them. We promised to smoke them together the next day. I'd smoke one with her this morning.

When I arrived, I felt the burden of my secret shrouding my shoulders, weighing me down. I put on my happy face for the residents of the transitional living home I worked at. Twelve men and women with AIDS lived at this facility; many of them were there to live out the rest of their lives, while others stayed until they got back on their feet after being homeless and learned how to manage their multiple medications. I was the house manager and occasionally sat outside to have a "butt break" with the residents as a way to connect. I wanted to beeline my way to my office, but like most mornings, Juan, one of the sicker residents, was sitting on the smoking porch, his long legs crossed and then nearly crossed again like a pretzel, so thin was his body. His deep, hollow eyes pierced mine, and as always, I was surprised at how they could still smile.

"Good morning, Colleen." His voice was like warm chocolate syrup slipping over a scoop of ice cream.

"Good morning, Juan. How are you today?" I often sat in on morning rounds and knew his body was failing. He was clearly dying.

"Oh, you know, my stomach feels better, but my head feels worse. Same old, same old. How are you?" He gazed directly into my eyes as he always did, unnerving me. They held something deep and knowing. I wanted to tell him what I was grappling with, wanted to think he could look into my heart and with his ghostly gaze extract some wisdom and courage that I felt I lacked.

"Oh, I've been better," I said. "But it's a gorgeous day and I'm here with you. What else could I want?"

"You got that right, sister!" he said with a wave of his hand and Broadway flair, revealing his flamboyant gay side.

We chatted a little more—just small talk—and then I went inside. Talking with Juan grounded me, made me feel just a little better.

What would he think if he knew I was pregnant? I imagined he would think life is precious and not to be lightly snuffed out.

I walked pass the small nursing station, which was built directly in the middle of the house so all the residents could have quick access to the staff. Windows lined the walls; when the two morning staff members saw me, they got up in a panic. Alice, the RN, came rushing out.

"Colleen, we need to talk. Mitch was at it again last night."

"Oh, really? Again? Okay, I'll talk to him." This is not what I wanted to hear this morning. Mitch, another resident, was loath to give up his marijuana and tried to secretly smoke in his room. I personally had no issue with pot smoking, but as the manager in charge of resident life, I had to enforce our policies. Illegal drugs were not allowed on our property. Alice filled me in on the details before I set off for my office. I didn't get far before I saw Kathy, the cook, bent over and digging in the fridge.

"Morning, Kathy."

"Huh?" Her head popped out of the fridge. "Oh, hi, Colleen. Hey, I'm glad you're here—smells like we have a dead animal in the basement. You might want to check out the air ducts today." She gave a little laugh. I could tell she was only too happy to pass this responsibility over to me.

"Oh, you're kidding. Yeah, I'll take care of it." The mounting responsibilities made me want a smoke to decompress.

Just down the short hallway from the kitchen was my office. When I stepped inside, I shut the door, not wanting any more problems to touch me right then. I saw the two green cigarettes sitting on my desk, tempting me. Cherie wouldn't be in for another hour, so I would force myself to wait. I sat down, put my head in my cupped hands, and pressed my fingers into my closed eyes to stifle the tears. I didn't feel happy. I didn't feel sad. I was simply overwhelmed. *I'm pregnant. What am I going to do?* The decision felt too big. When would I finally say yes to having a child? Did I want a child? My past suggested I didn't, but at least some small part of my heart was saying yes. How could I say no to this union of Mark and myself? How could I say no to a part of the future we'd planned together? But this was too soon. I wasn't prepared. We didn't have a house yet. We hadn't even *thought* of buying a house. I was thirty-five years old and had grown up a lot, but in the face of this reality, I felt as emotionally unprepared for this as I had at twenty.

When Cherie arrived at work and came into my office, I held up the two green cigarettes. "I think it's time we smoke them, don't you?" My mouth was watering.

"Absolutely. Why wait?" Cherie exuded her usual calm demeanor; she was unflappable. I wished I had some of her calmness to call upon right then.

We went out to the empty smoking porch. I was glad for the quiet. I wanted to smoke what might be my last cigarette in peace. I always told myself the one thing that could make me quit smoking was pregnancy. While I wasn't ready to fully accept this pregnancy, I also couldn't pretend it wasn't happening. I knew this had to be my last cigarette until I figured this out.

I wanted to tell Cherie I was pregnant; she and I had worked together for over six months and had developed a sweet friendship. I was bursting to talk this out with her, to hear myself think, to get this volcanic energy out of my body, but I knew I had to wait. This decision required a longer conversation with Mark, so I kept my own counsel. We lit up our green cigarettes, giggling. Between the smoke and our casual conversation, I settled down and realized I could actually get through the day until I could go home to Mark. When I put the cigarette out, I did so sadly, already feeling the ache of the loss.

After work, I drove home as fast as I could. I couldn't wait to hug Mark and feel his quiet strength. We decided to get out of the city the next day, which was Saturday, to think about what to do. We took the ferry across Puget Sound to Port Townsend, a quaint artsy community west of Seattle. The ferry ride alone was calming and centering: Mt. Rainier, the sentinel of Seattle, loomed in the background; seagulls followed the ferry, making a ruckus as they screamed for tidbits of food; and the boat rocked gently over the small swells. Port Townsend was calming, too, and its slow-paced small-town charm, turn-of-the-century brick buildings, and whimsically painted Victorian houses seemed to shed the outermost layer of city cares. We bought sandwiches at a local deli and took them to the beach a mile outside of town. I watched parents and their children throwing Frisbees in the wind and making sand castles on the beach. Families gallivanted along the water's edge, and everyone looked so happy.

Mark and I didn't talk a lot. We sat together with our private thoughts. I knew that since we'd gotten married, Mark's default mode was to assume we would have a baby someday. But I also knew he hoped to travel before that happened. If we went forward with this pregnancy, life would change as much for him as it would for me. He would have to adjust to the idea of becoming the breadwinner for a family instead of making money for the next adventure.

As for me, I was both repulsed at the thought of having another abortion, and tempted to go that route again. I thought about the ritual of carrying the two little swaddled bundles around in my pocket that I had done two years earlier. And though much of my burden had abated after that, my choices still weighed heavy on my heart during dark moments. I didn't want to carry that kind of weight again.

I watched a little girl across the beach start to wail after she fell off a log and skinned her knee. Her mother was so gentle with her, comforting her with a hug and cooing soft words. *I want to be a gentle, kind mother,* I thought. I saw a ten-year-old boy playing catch with his dad in the field behind us. *Mark will make a great dad.* The idea of Mark being a father filled my chest with warmth.

After sitting on the beach for an hour, the wind gusting occasionally, I finally mustered the courage to say it. "We're going to have a baby, aren't we?" I looked at Mark, trying to gauge how he felt.

"It looks like it, honey. Are you okay with that?" He sounded relaxed. He looked relaxed. Maybe this was going to be good.

"I'm terrified," I admitted "But I'm okay with it. How about you?" I took his hand.

"This wasn't what I expected right now, but yeah, I'm good with it." I saw by his expression, the faith in his eyes, that this was true.

We hugged for a long while, my head against his chest. I felt safe hearing his heartbeat. I reveled in the feeling of warmth that flooded my chest and the spark of excitement that I finally allowed to ignite.

When we got home, I called my mom. "Hi, Mom. Guess what? We're looking to buy a house."

"Really? So soon? Are you sure you can afford it?" I could hear the concern in her voice.

"Well . . . actually, pretty soon this duplex is going to be too small for us." I paused. Waited. I knew it would sink in if I just gave it time. Silence.

"Oh, Colleen, really? REALLY? Oh, honey! Really?" She was squealing.

"Yeah, Mom, really."

And then I started to cry. I could finally tell my mom I was pregnant. Finally. My heart wanted to burst with joy. I had nine nieces and nephews by then, and I had seen Mom hold each one of them.

"Sweetest heart of Jesus," she said between clenched teeth, so big was her love. Now Mom would whisper the same loving words to my child. It was finally my turn.

17
• ● •
GETTING BIGGER

Since I'd gotten myself into therapy and started to peel away the layers of grief, I thought I was making good progress toward a happy life. And since I'd forgiven myself for my two abortions, and forgiven Harvey, I felt I was free to think of myself as more than an amputee. I was a woman who could fall in love—and become a mother. They say there are five stages of grief: denial, bargaining, anger, depression, and acceptance. What they don't say is that with any big, life-altering loss, the layers of grief repeat—and repeat again. For someone who loses something significant, every period of healing is likely to be followed by another loss. Becoming pregnant, and ultimately becoming a mother, was about to throw me into the hardest learning curve I'd encountered since my accident eighteen years earlier. And the stakes were very high. If I didn't find my way through the darkness that was about to envelop me, there were now others, whose lives were intimately tied to mine, who would be impacted negatively.

The problem began the minute I smoked my last cigarette—the green one I'd shared with Cherie on the porch at work. After Mark's and my decision to move forward with the pregnancy, morning sickness quickly settled in, the kind that lingers at low levels throughout the day. Having a cigarette crossed my mind many times, but these were thoughts, not true cravings. What I missed wasn't the cigarette as much as the excuse for a break, the chance to let go of everything and go back to myself. I was surprised the cravings weren't as much physical as they were emotional. I felt like I had lost a friend. The friend who joined me for my pity parties, the friend I went to when I wanted to hide from my sadness, anger, and fear.

So many decades of denying one's feelings through the crutch of a bad habit is not easily undone by a couple of years in therapy. I replaced one oral fixation with another: food. The sweeter, the better. Kathy, the cook at work, often left a plate of homemade cookies on the kitchen counter for the residents and staff to snack on. Prior to pregnancy, I'd pass them by in favor of a cigarette. After I quit smoking, I indulged in the cookies with a vengeance, and for the first time since I'd lost my leg, I started gaining weight. Really gaining weight.

Having spent the previous eighteen years watching my weight, I was surprised at how easily I loosened my grip. I didn't care anymore, but I should have. I wasn't your run-of-the-mill pregnant woman who could take time off from watching her figure while she grew a baby. I was a pregnant woman whose life only functioned because she had a well-fitting prosthetic leg. I was a woman who would be grounded if her stump outgrew her prosthesis.

My diet had never been good: coffee and a cigarette was my typical breakfast, followed by a scone at my desk later in the morning and then dinner out. But I did limit my sweets. Candy bars were a rarity in my pre-pregnancy life. Milkshakes? Maybe twice a year. And donuts were nearly taboo. Now I was indulging, partly because I was hungry and partly because I'd lost the solace of smoking.

Weight gain is the nemesis for any amputee with a prosthesis that attaches by suction, such as mine does. I knew I was playing with the devil by eating so many sweets. I could feel the pounds adding on, but I rationalized it as "baby weight," and I kept eating for two.

One morning halfway through my pregnancy, I tried to put on my leg and could barely squeeze in. My stump throbbed from being stuffed into the socket of my prosthetic leg. It felt like a size-nine foot crammed into a size-six shoe. Walking around at work that whole week was barely manageable. Navigating my own home was starting to become difficult. At the grocery store one afternoon, I eyed the scooter carts from the corner of my eye but quickly dismissed them. *Those are for old ladies*, I thought. *I wouldn't be caught dead in one.* Instead, I limped around the store, bearing my weight on the grocery cart, fighting back tears of pain.

I set my mind to try to limit my consumption, but found I didn't have the willpower. So I had a temporary prosthetic leg made to accommodate my increasingly large stump. Making a good-fitting leg takes up to three months and requires a stable weight. I had neither the luxury to wait three months nor a stable weight. Making the pregnancy leg took longer than we expected.

When I went in for my first fitting and looked at the leg my prosthetist handed me, I was confused. It took a moment to register what was amiss: he had made the leg for the wrong side of my body. It was at this point that I began to feel myself start to unravel.

I became furious with him and almost threw the leg across the room. He felt horrible, and told me he would rush a new one and get it to me in a week. But I didn't have a week; I could barely move anymore. I went home and sobbed in Mark's arms. I had not felt so helpless since the first weeks after my accident. I wanted to disintegrate into a little ball of smoke and let the wind blow me away.

Thus, as my body was making my son's heart, my own heart was breaking. As I was making his chubby little legs, I was losing my own leg again. And with it, this time, I was also losing my hard-won identity as a capable, disciplined, functioning woman.

Every four or five years I had replaced my prosthetic leg, and the process was always difficult. I'd never been able to squelch the anger that threatened to erupt when I had to change legs. Everything feels different on a new leg—not just walking, but also sitting on a toilet, getting in and out of a car, and the way my clothes fit around my hips. Each new leg had the latest technology, so there was always an incentive to set aside my distaste for the adjustment period and to accommodate the improvements.

But the pregnancy leg was different than the other legs I'd had. This leg was archaic. With nothing more than a bucket for a socket, the new leg fit too loosely over my flesh and fastened onto my body with a six-inch-wide black neoprene belt that wrapped around my baby bump to hold it in place. There was no suction, so now my stump felt like a size-nine foot sloshing around inside a size-twelve shoe. I knew this was the only answer to my weight-gain problem, but I immediately hated this leg with the same intensity I envied every skinny pregnant woman I encountered.

Every morning after my shower, I reluctantly slipped my stump into the leg's socket and tightly wrapped the neoprene belt around my increasingly large belly. I worried about my baby as I cinched the belt tightly around him. I worried my belly would swell beyond the size of the belt and then I wouldn't have any leg to wear. I started wearing the pregnancy leg in July, just as Seattle entered summer; the black neoprene belt, besides feeling like a corset, increased my rising body temperature.

One July evening, feeling heavy and low, I took my old prosthetic leg to the basement to "retire" it. I sat at the bottom of the stairs, holding the leg I had worn during the previous five years of activity and adventure. I took some markers and drew symbols on it depicting the many experiences I had during the five years I wore it: kayak trips, hiking trips, my solo trip to Mexico. Then I gave way to my grief—one more layer of grief as the onion lost another layer. Pregnancy was taking all these things—and with them, my identity—from me. I felt like such a failure. Of all people, I should have done everything possible to keep my weight down. I was giving up more than just my leg; I was giving up a way of life that I'd worked very hard to establish. Instead of sitting in my kayak paddling between islands, I was now sitting most evenings on my couch watching TV. Instead of walking through the woods, I was barely able to walk down the interminably long aisles in the grocery store. Sadness enveloped me. Was I giving up my freedom, my active lifestyle, and my joyful connections with nature for good? I didn't know how to be truly disabled, as in un-able to live my life as I'd established it. I'd learned over the years how to adapt activities so I could still do them, but I didn't know how to live with not being able to do those activities at all. Who would I be now that walking was painful in this new way? I'd been through so many iterations of legs over the years and had encountered easily a hundred different kinds of pain, but nothing like the pain of walking in the pregnancy leg. Instead of my stump being securely held, it slid around, causing skin breakdown and sores. How would I be the self who could walk a rugged trail or ski down a mountain when I was rubbed so raw and wobbling so awkwardly?

The more physically limited I became, the more I wanted to hide my feelings in something chemical, so conditioned was I. Sugar had replaced cigarettes, and I felt caught on a merry-go-round whenever I consumed the very thing that was causing my excessive weight gain in the first place. I didn't realize it wasn't the cigarettes or the sugar that were causing my pain. It was the feelings I was so desperately trying not to feel. I was lost in a deep void of grief. Even my armor couldn't protect me from this.

As I sat holding my leg in the basement, Mark came to the top of the stairs. "You okay?" he said.

I snapped at him, "What does it look like? I'm a useless, one-legged woman."

"Do you want company?"

"No!" I screamed. I was embarrassed, both at my sniveling and my little ritual. I couldn't see his green eyes from where I sat, but I knew I'd hurt him.

"I'll be up here if you want to talk," he said and then walked back upstairs and away from the doorway.

I put my head in my hands, convinced that besides becoming useless, I'd also just shown myself to be a pathetic bitch—Mark would become afraid to reach out toward me if I didn't get hold of myself. We had only been married for about a year, and he had never seen me like this. He only knew the confident, capable Colleen. Neither one of us had expected me to change so much with the pregnancy. Neither one of us knew quite what to do with me. I wrapped the leg in a blanket, put it on a shelf, ascended the basement stairs, and descended deeper into a lonely, dark place of helplessness.

After two abortions, I was finally pregnant, and I wanted to be happy. I wanted to enjoy this experience. But for all the milestones I experienced during pregnancy, I couldn't let go into the kind of joy I'd watched my sisters and sisters-in-law enjoy with theirs. When I saw my baby's image on the ultrasound, I wanted to feel connected and excited, but I felt his little budding life as the loss of my independence, my identity—the loss of me. I wasn't the woman I had spent so many years becoming. And I didn't know yet that every person's life is a series of re-visionings and re-makings. I thought I was alone in this upheaval.

After just a few weeks with the new leg, I did the unimaginable: with tears welling in my eyes, I dug out my crutches from the depths of the closet. The same crutches I'd used in the weeks after the accident. The same crutches I'd used walking around the high school hallways, looking like a freak. The same crutches which had drawn stares, and which made me swear I could feel the disgust rising in people's bellies. This crappy leg *and* the crutches, mixed with my weight gain, lack of mobility, and *Goddamn it, I even had zits again,* made me feel I was back to square one. Who was Colleen? Nothing but a childish beached whale sitting on the couch every night after work and stuffing her face with comfort food.

18

· ● ·

MY SAFETY NET

Our one-bedroom duplex, just half a block from the Puget Sound, was not going to be big enough for three of us. Images of a baby crying in the middle of the night and waking our neighbor were enough reason to ask the question: "Do you think we should talk to a realtor?" I couldn't believe we were actually considering buying a house. After all, hadn't Mark and I believed we'd escape the conventional path most couples walked? I felt an internal tug-of-war between wanting to do life differently and wanting to take the traditional route that felt familiar and comfortable. If I was walking into this pregnancy with the huge unknown of how it would affect my leg, I needed to know something was secure. A home of our own would do the trick.

"Yeah, we can talk to her and see what she says," Mark said. "But I don't think we can afford much of a house. We're still paying off the wedding." I heard the concern and weight in his voice. Mark analyzed decisions and took a while to do so. I was more intuitive in my decision-making process. If something felt right, I'd often just go for it. Because our marriage was new, we were learning how to mesh our styles.

"Well, let's just talk to her," I said. This was a big step. Aside from saying yes to the pregnancy, buying a house was as big as it got in my world. The only thing I could commit to at this point was talking about it with a realtor.

Just a few days later, we did talk to her. And in two more days, we were in her Volvo, driving around Seattle neighborhoods looking at charming two- and three-bedroom houses. I only remember one of those houses, the one we decided to buy. All the houses we had viewed before that one "had potential," we told the realtor, which meant we left each viewing feeling a little grungier than when we had walked in. The house we bought was adorable.

Exuding charm, it sat on a corner in an older neighborhood. The house itself was almost perfect. The only concern I had was that we would live just three blocks from a busy arterial. On the other hand, three blocks in the other direction was the school where Luke would watch the "ball boys" practice football drills in the fall, and just beyond that was the neighborhood park where he would swing with delight. So, despite the busy street, we decided to put in an offer on the house.

Due to the housing boom in Seattle, once we made the decision to put in an offer, our realtor swooped us into her office to write it up. Urgency was the tone of our meeting as she scribbled the amount of our down payment and contingencies. As we were signing our names to the multiple documents, she jokingly told us what *mortgage* meant in French: "death pledge." I wished she hadn't told us that. Sweat formed on my brow, and my handwriting became shaky, but we were unflagging in our decision. Soon Mark and I were the proud owners of our first home together.

I was told to anticipate that our first year of marriage would be hard, but I didn't expect that I would be reconfiguring my identity at the same time that I was figuring how to meld my life with someone else's. Most people don't understand how much marriage can throw a person's identity up in the air, at least briefly. But for me, not only was I adding "wife" and "homeowner" to my self-perception, but also "disabled" in a way that had never occurred to me before.

I was worried about how the difficulties of my pregnancy

would be central to the development of the foundation of our marriage. During our whirlwind courtship and engagement, our main challenges had been making decisions about the wedding, but those negotiations didn't prepare either of us for the challenge of dealing with my growing state of despondency as the pregnancy progressed.

At the height of summer, Mark got a call from his college roommate, Jay. He was in Seattle on business and wanted to meet me and take us to dinner. We met at a restaurant by Green Lake, a popular local gathering place. Sitting on the patio under an umbrella, I drank a "near beer" and sulked while Mark and Jay drank real beer and caught up with each other. When Jay tried to talk to me, I uncharacteristically shut him down.

It wasn't like me to be rude, but I couldn't access the small-talking, chitchatty part of myself. Sure, I resented that I couldn't languish in the heat of the evening and get a little buzzed, but mostly I resented that my husband seemed so carefree while I carried the weight of my loss of "Colleen" as I'd created her over the years. Mark was about to become a parent just as I was, but he sat with his buddy catching up on old times, unchanged from the days when he and Jay had lived together. I, on the other hand, was being emptied by this pregnancy of everything I thought I was: energetic, mobile, adventurous, and physically spry.

I was still learning about self-regulating my emotions from Lynn, and that night wasn't the only night I didn't do so well. I often felt like a victim of my own feelings. Lynn told me that when we suffer a trauma, a part of us is emotionally stunted at the age at which the trauma occurred. That night at dinner—as well as on many other nights—I had acted like a brooding teenager. Another part of me looked on, urging me to grow up, but that part wasn't very strong yet. The teenager won out.

Later at home Mark asked, "Honey, you seemed distant and rude tonight? Was something wrong?"

"No," I replied, aware that Mark must have been confused by my behavior. "I just didn't feel like I belonged. You two were catching up, and I'm just a fat pregnant lady."

"But I wanted Jay to get to know you." I heard a small resentment in his voice and I saw that worse than having missed the opportunity to get to know Jay, I wasn't contributing to our marriage in the way I had envisioned or hoped. I simply didn't have the energy and wherewithal to give much of myself to the relationship. In this first year of marriage, Mark and I were putting the foundation of our future into place, brick by brick. I was failing him, myself, and our marriage by adding bricks forged with my sadness and anger. I could sense some of the bricks Mark was adding to our foundation were going to be fired in the oven of his resentment. I only hoped that our love would be strong enough for us to keep building, even if there were a few faulty bricks in the structure.

Things would get harder before they would get easier, unfortunately. Many nights I came home from work in tears. It was difficult to hold my emotions in check all day, and by the time I got home, I was like a wound-up rubber band flying through the air. I tried to keep these feelings from Mark, knowing I was like a pressure cooker close to blowing my top. One night I came home from work, threw myself onto our bed, and started sobbing. Mark rushed into the room, paused, and then sat on the bed. "Honey, what's going on?"

How could I explain to him that the deeper I peeled into the onion of my grief, the more tears there seemed to be? "I'm just so sad. I didn't expect this. This hurts so much." Mark lay down next to me.

"You mean your leg hurts?" I could tell he was trying to understand and I was frustrated that he didn't. How could he, of course? But it's so hard to feel misunderstood and unknown by the person you need most in the world.

"Not just my leg. It's everything." He simply spooned his body around mine. He didn't tell me it would be okay; he just let me cry.

He didn't shush me. He just squeezed me when another wave of tears surged through my body. Unlike so many other people in my life over the years, Mark didn't ask me to step up to the plate and push my sadness aside so he could be okay. He just stayed with me *in* it, even though it was clearly hard for him.

I was finally safe in someone's arms, able to express the sadness that I had harbored for so many years. I had always feared that if I gave in to my emotions I'd freefall into a black hole of sadness, but there I was, cradled by the safety net of Mark's love. Because I had him, I was finally able to utter the words I had been scared to say for eighteen years.

"I can't do this, honey. This is too hard." I'd never said that—never admitted that I wanted to give up on myself. Mark just listened. "Why did this happen to me?" He offered no response. I no longer thought in terms of God. I wasn't asking why God had taken my leg, but I was asking a cosmic question for certain. Why me? Why was this my journey? And Mark simply held me as the question that had been burning in my heart was finally asked aloud.

I thought I had healed the wounds in my heart when I'd forgiven myself and Harvey. But my pregnancy revealed how many crevices in the wound were still raw. My trauma, as all trauma is, was nuanced, rich, deep, multi-dimensional, and very, very tender. My physical pain nimbly picked at the scab, the thin layer of illusion, until my heart was bleeding with sadness once again. Could I ever find real, long-lasting relief and healing? How? Who could offer that to me? If this kind, loving man beside me could not heal me, who could?

In August, when I was six months pregnant, Mark and I took a trip down the Oregon coast. Getting through Seattle traffic was easy that day, but the traffic in Olympia, an hour south of Seattle, was at a standstill. We didn't have air-conditioning in our car, so I rolled down my window. The air was heavy from the heat and the exhaust spewing from the cars ahead. My stump became very uncomfortable. Sitting in the car was almost unbearable. Between grunts, groans, and moans, I shifted my body in the seat, no easy maneuver with my growing belly and clunky prosthetic leg. I felt like a prisoner in my own body, and now I felt captive in my small car. I wanted to throw something. And here is where my final, healing shift began.

"*Aaaaggghhh!* I have to get out of this car!" I groaned.

Mark, already sensing my obvious discomfort, was gentle. "Honey, the next exit is about three miles away. Can you hold on till then?"

I didn't want this to be his fault, but I had to direct this roiling energy somewhere, or I might implode. I raised my voice in angry panic. "Three miles? I can't wait three miles!"

"I can't get over for a while, can you hold on?" he asked again cautiously.

But my leg was burning all the way from the end of my stump to my crotch, and my heart was pounding too fast. We were on our last trip as a couple before the baby was born. I'd wanted this trip to be a good chance for us to connect with each other, but suddenly my irritation and anxiety felt too big for the car—too big for my body. I simply could not get it under control.

I worried about my baby's life forming in my cauldron of anger. What was it like for him to begin his life in my hell? Was my boiling blood pulsing through his veins? Was my rage infused in the amniotic fluid surrounding his body? Once he was born and cried his first cry, would his tears echo the tears I'd shed during his gestation, or would they be tears of relief from finally being free from his nine-month prison? This thought was almost too much for me.

I heard a scream of utter frustration and bitterness erupt from my own throat. And then, "Goddamn it!" I shouted. "Just keep driving. Forget it."

"What?" Mark looked at me, perplexed.

I answered through clenched teeth. "I said forget it." I didn't know how to let this frustrated rage go. Like having a vice grip around my heart, I felt constricted by its power.

And then, in one of those rare but welcome light-bulb moments, like when long division suddenly made sense back in elementary school, I remembered Lynn's words to me, something she had been repeating for months: "You get to take care of you." I recalled what we'd been practicing in our sessions. And I shut my eyes. I started to take slow deep breaths the way she'd taught me. *Just breathe, Colleen. In. Out. In. Out.*

Breathing was akin to peeling another layer of the onion. Once I focused inward on my breath, I felt the shift. The anger and fear loosened its grip on my heart, which then opened to the sadness. Always under my anger was sadness. At first I felt a flood of regret and shame for my outburst; then I was consumed with sorrow—for hurting Mark, for my physical pain, for being a one-legged pregnant woman. But I had to acknowledge there was a new layer to my feelings this time. Each time my sorrow was cared for, each time space was made for it, new colors of it broke through.

This pregnancy brought its own joy, but it also held unique challenges. I was confronted once again with the limits of my body. How could this not make me sad? I had to face the reality that losing my leg those many years ago continued to adversely affect my life at every new stage I entered. Who would not grieve over this? Sadness washed over me in the car for all the pain, anger, and inconvenience of my pregnancy, and how those negative feelings tainted the joy I wanted to feel. But I felt a difference from the sadness I'd felt earlier in the peeling of the onion. Today, in this car, I would be gentle with my anger and grief if only for this moment.

I tried to patch things up with Mark by apologizing through my tears, but I knew some damage had been done. If I didn't learn how to be in a healthy relationship with my sadness, I was going to slowly break his trust in me. He was like a volcanologist, studying my mood and tone, trying to determine when I'd explode again, but

I was too unpredictable for his untrained eye. I didn't want this for him; I was going to need to take my healing seriously.

The ocean worked her magic. Being close to the water that took my father's life so many years ago was like being in church. As the crashing waves ebbed back into the ocean, my sadness followed— coming and going at will.

One afternoon, Mark took a run on the beach. As I sat on a log watching him, he took my breath away. Because he was wearing shorts, I could see the muscles in his legs flex and soften, flex and soften. I marveled at the beauty of the human leg: the muscular thigh, the adaptable knee, the curvaceous calf, the flexible ankle, and the precious foot. He glided over the sand so easily. My throat constricted, and I heard myself moan. He was so beautiful. I wanted to enter his body and *be* him as he ran over the sand.

Mark finished his run and sat next to me on the log. I decided to open up to him, hoping my honesty would help stitch together the rift my anger had created.

"Honey," I asked nervously, "what kind of mother am I going to be if I can't run on the beach with our kids? I want to take our kids backpacking, but I can hardly walk through the grocery store."

Mark took my hand. "Colleen, things will get better. You will come through this. I know this isn't the pregnancy you hoped for, but you're doing a great job."

"I wish I could run with you. It's going to be so hard to not be able to run with our children." Here was the crux of my fear. What if I never regained my mobility? Was I going to disable everyone's life in my family? Keeping company with the ocean had led me into the center of my greatest worry: Would I hurt those I loved most with my inability to be other than what I was? Would I be an insufficient mother and harm my own child?

"Honey, stop right there. We need to take this a step at a time. What you're doing right now is the most important thing: you are creating a human being." The baby punctuated his point with a strong kick. And again, I closed my eyes and breathed in and out, working very hard to stay in the moment—this moment with my little family.

Back home, when we decorated the baby's room, I felt like I did when Mark and I were falling in love: full of anticipation to get to know the person who would inhabit this room, our world, my heart. I felt like I was living an emotional game of ping-pong—anger and sadness on one side of the net, excitement and joy on the other—but I was beginning to breathe through all of it.

In spite of all the years that I tried to control my environment and my activities, this baby was already becoming a teacher. I was learning that I couldn't control everything. I had been putting my efforts in the wrong place. Instead of controlling my outer world, I was learning that it was my inner world that I could—and should—control.

19

• ● •

A PART OF GOD

I was two weeks late. I had quit work a week before my due date, desperately wanting my pregnancy to be over and to take the next step into the world of motherhood. My days were spent alone watching movies and futzing around the house in the afternoon waiting for Mark to come home. The "nesting" was complete; I just needed my little baby. For as much angst as I had about the next phase of life, I was even more excited, and being excited felt good.

During the five years before Mark and I married, I'd studied medicinal herbology. Now, the garden in my new backyard provided many of the herbs I used; others I gathered in local parks. Homemade tinctures and salves were prepared and waiting both for labor and post-labor pain and discomfort. I wasn't a medical practitioner by any stretch, but common sense led me to believe that delivering a baby did not necessarily warrant medical intervention. Women, even women with disabilities, had been having babies long before modern medicine came along. In spite of all the ways my body had betrayed me over the years, I somehow hoped that it could get me through labor without making it a medical ordeal. Wherever this faith came from, I took comfort in it.

I wanted to have a home birth, not only to bring my baby into the world gently, but also to avoid the hospital. I would be forever grateful to modern medicine for saving my life, but I didn't want the lingering scent of sterility and pain in a hospital to be a part of my birth experience. Home births weren't covered by our insurance, however, and Mark was nervous about possible complications that could require medical intervention. So we compromised: I found a nurse-midwife who worked in the hospital. She espoused the midwife philosophy—that each woman has the right to a natural birth—and she was also armed with all the interventions of allopathic medicine, including an MD. If anything came up, all she had to do was contact the doctor who was on call. During the course of pregnancy, she and I had talked about my birth plan, and I felt strongly that I didn't want to use any drugs.

A few years ago, not long after I started working with Lynn, she had suggested I visit Catherine, a naturopath, to help deal with the phantom pain I had experienced ever since I lost my leg. During the course of the six months I saw the naturopath, she prescribed a variety of herbal remedies. She would start off each session by asking questions about any differences I felt as a result of the remedy I was currently taking, and by reviewing any changes in physical symptoms and how I felt emotionally. No matter how casually I mentioned a topic, she'd investigate each one, leaving no stone unturned. From her perspective, everything was intertwined; she was a firm believer in the mind–body connection. Her matter-of-fact demeanor would instantly shift to a warm and fuzzy one the second she sensed any emotion coming from me. During one session, through my shame, I confessed to her that I smoked. Without judgment, she asked me some questions. I explained I'd started smoking a few months after my accident and that I particularly craved cigarettes when I was upset.

She asked permission to talk me through a guided meditation. I had used guided imagery frequently in my twenties during my quest for deeper spiritual understanding, so I quickly agreed. I lay on her exam table, and after a few minutes of relaxing and deep breathing, Catherine asked me to move backward in time until I reached my earliest memory. I was two years old, holding on to my father's hand as we ascended the thirteen steps in our new house.

Then she asked me to go back even further and further still, until I was back in my mother's womb.

I felt myself, small and scrunched up, floating in a dark, liquid world. I heard the whooshing of my mother's blood surrounding me. In the distance, I heard Catherine's voice telling me I was ready to leave my mother's womb.

I felt the contractions. My body, forced to shift and move, was squeezed into new positions. I was confused and didn't know what was happening. I sensed time passing, and the contractions became stronger. I panicked and felt afraid: I didn't want to leave my home. Then a sudden feeling washed through me, and I felt different: somewhat agitated, but I didn't feel afraid anymore. I moved through the birth canal and saw my mother's beautiful face and heard her familiar voice.

Catherine explained to me that the drugs they used during my mother's labor were my first introduction to the concept of using a drug during stress to relieve fear and grief. Given what I experienced in Catherine's office, I vowed to avoid planting that same seed of a crutch in my own children, if I could help it.

Thus, my choice to forego drugs during childbirth wasn't merely ethical; it was driven by a deeper concern for my child. It was a decision I'd made even before Mark and I had known one another.

During the last month of pregnancy, I saw Nancy, my midwife, every week so she could measure the baby and determine if my cervix was starting to open. Once we hit the two-weeks-overdue date, she decided to gently induce labor using Pitocin, a synthetic form of the naturally occurring hormone oxytocin, which stimulates contractions. Nancy assured me no harm would come to my baby. I knew my baby was getting big, and if he didn't come out soon, I might require a C-section. I desperately wanted to have my baby naturally, so I agreed to the Pitocin. Mark and I went to the hospital in the morning, and I was hooked up to the IV drip. After an hour, Nancy sent us home with instructions to have a good lunch for strength and to take a walk around the block to help induce labor.

On the way home, Mark and I had Greek food for lunch, a choice I would later regret as I spewed my heavily laden garlic breath throughout the hospital room. After we returned home, I felt small cramps, but having never been through labor before, I had a hard time deciphering if they were labor's beginning, a bad reaction to lunch, or nerves. We decided to do whatever we could to help the baby along, so we took Nancy's prescribed walk.

I crossed the threshold of my front door and looked down the four steps leading to the sidewalk and then down the interminably long block. In the six months Mark and I had lived in our new house, I had never explored my own neighborhood on foot. Though I'd driven past the park three blocks away, I never stopped to see where my child would one day play. I had no idea how important that park would become to us once our little one was old enough to walk. And right then, on the precipice of labor, three blocks to me might as well have been a walk to the moon. But I wanted to do as Nancy had said, so I hobbled down the stairs and, with Mark next to me, began to limp down the road.

We didn't know the gender of our baby, and I was busting with excitement to meet the creature who had turned my life upside down. So there I was, walking down the sidewalk, seeing front yards and houses I'd never noticed as I'd driven by them on my way to work each day. The houses were all vintage 1920s bungalows, and old, soggy leaves littered the yards. While the earth was in the depths of autumn's decay, I was ready to bring forth new life. As we were nearing the dark time of the year, I could sense a new light coming into my life.

I walked slowly, leaning heavily on my crutches, fearful of inducing labor and yet desperate to do so. Mark walked quietly beside me, feeling his own fear and excitement. Pain was my constant companion now. My relationship with it was complicated, but familiar. As a way of preparing myself for what was to come, I kept telling myself the pain in my leg was likely small peanuts compared to the pain of labor. My midwife had every confidence that I could manage it, even when I voiced my fears to her.

"Do you think I can do natural childbirth with just one leg?"

"Colleen, the part of your body that will deliver a baby is intact. Childbirth is childbirth. Your body will know what to do. I'll be there to help if there are any complications, but the loss of your leg won't be the cause of them."

That was reassuring, but how did I know she really understood my situation. "Have you ever worked with an amputee before?" I'd challenged her.

"No, but I don't really see it as an issue." She had delivered many babies and had seen many situations. In fact, she seemed surer of me than I was of myself. I had lost some of my fly-down-the-mountain-with-wind-whipping-through-my-hair self-confidence over the last nine months and was dubious about her confidence in my abilities. In any new activity I learned, I usually needed to teach my teachers how to help me. Except for my skiing and soccer coaches, I'd rarely encountered a teacher or coach who had taught an amputee before. I wanted to believe the loss of my leg wouldn't make my birth experience harder, but how could I—or Nancy—know if that would be the case?

I had walked only two blocks down the road before my whole stump began throbbing. I was sweating from the exertion. It was on the tip of my tongue to ask Mark to go get the car and take me home. But I knew this walk might help me get the labor started, so instead, I just signaled to Mark to hold still for a moment so I could lean against him, close my eyes, and breathe through the worst of it. The tight knot in my stomach resisting the pain was loosened as I heard my old physical therapist's voice in my head, spurring me on: "Atta girl, you can do it!" *Okay, yes, I can do this*, I thought. This wasn't as hard as taking my first steps in the hospital. I took a deep breath and felt Mark's gentle presence beside me. I opened my eyes, transferred my weight back onto my crutches, and kept walking.

The walk worked. Labor began in earnest, and I spent the next ten hours watching a movie, preparing Christmas gifts, and taking a bath to soothe the cramps. Mark lit candles all over the bathroom and sat on the toilet as I soaked, my belly protruding like a barren island. Then, finally, it was time.

Labor was in full swing shortly after we settled into the hospital room. I changed into a nightgown, unstrapped the six-inch neoprene belt attached to my prosthetic leg, and removed it. I landed on the bed like a beached whale. The fifty pounds I'd gained during pregnancy had stripped away all my grace and finesse, but I'd made it here. And I was as ready as I could be.

After another hour of labor, and a long time of trying to reposition myself on the bed to help alleviate the searing pain of the contractions, my old nemesis, fear, crept in. The absence of my second leg and how it impaired my movements was glaringly obvious. Without the leverage of my other leg, readjusting my position was difficult, and turning onto my side on my own was nearly impossible. I was limited to one position: lying on my back. *Am I really going to be able to do this?* I fretted.

After a few hours of watching me struggle, Nancy drew me a warm bath in a deep tub. Transferring me from the bed to the wheelchair in the midst of my pain was a Herculean effort on everyone's part. Just sitting me up took the three of us; Mark straddled me from behind, pushing me forward, while the midwife pulled my arms from in front. Once I was upright, I stopped to allow another contraction to pass and then turned my body and slid my leg over the bed, near the wheelchair. Mark was right next to me, guiding me as I stood up, pivoted my body, and plopped into the chair. Anyone who says birth contractions happen in the uterus is telling lies. I felt my whole body contracting.

While the labor was agonizing, I had an odd relief in feeling a new kind of pain, a productive pain. The pain during pregnancy had only worn me down; this pain I felt I could transcend. My only job was to deal with the pain and do what the midwife told me. I didn't have to walk; I didn't have to focus on anything or take care of anyone. All I had to do was get through each contraction.

Mark stayed in the hospital room while I soaked in the warmth of the bath. The lights were low, and Nancy sat quietly beside the tub. It was two a.m. I floated, exhausted, in and out of ethereal consciousness until the next contraction plunged my awareness back into the tub. Nancy gently coached me through each one, and then when it passed, I slipped away again. Images of women washed over me in my hazy dream state; an infinite procession of women, chanting softly, formed a ribbon of support and guidance around my body. I sensed these women were everlasting, from the beginning of time. They infused me with the confidence and wisdom inherent in a woman's body. I relaxed in the understanding that my missing leg truly didn't matter, not now. Not here. Just as Nancy had promised, my body knew what to do.

But then suddenly it did matter. Suddenly I was yanked out of my gentle reverie. The ribbon of support disappeared, and my left leg started to cramp hard due to its bent position in the small Japanese-style tub. Nancy grew concerned and called a nurse to help haul me out of the bath, into the wheelchair, and back into my room. After measuring my cervix, Nancy determined the warm water had slowed down my dilation.

I watched her face and could see her trying to hide her worry. I was gripped with fear when I realized I had to stay in bed and deal with labor outside of the water that had been so comforting only moments ago. The intensity of my contractions now doubled without the water's soothing effects. I closed my eyes and tried to conjure up the image of my flotilla of women, but they were gone. Doubt surfaced again. *Can I really do this?*

There are times in our lives when we fear we are not up to the tasks required of us—moments when feel we are not made of enough toughness to face our circumstances. In this moment, I felt weak and small. I just wanted this all to stop.

But from somewhere inside of me, perhaps from a mother's fierce protective instinct for her child, my resolve surfaced. My decision was still clear. I wouldn't use drugs. I opened the file drawers in my mind and pulled out images of strength from my past: my first backpacking trip after the accident, playing soccer on one leg, my five-mile backpacking trip, snowshoeing, kayaking in five-foot swells on the Pacific. I had been physically challenged before, and I'd always been faced with doubt about whether or not I could really do it. But I never failed. *Yes, I can do this.*

I retreated into my own dark world behind my closed eyes, managing the pain in my leg, moving beyond the ache to a place of calm. I conjured up images of the mountains, the sea, places that brought me comfort. The dead weight of pain in my leg never left, but I stayed with it. A few hours passed. I was unaware of the clock or anything outside of my body except for Mark wiping the sweat from my brow now and again.

The midwife measured my cervix again. "Colleen, if you'd like to get back into a tub, you're far enough along. We have a bigger tub, so you can stretch your leg."

The second bath didn't bring reprieve from the pain like the first bath did. I was too far along in labor. The intensity and frequency of my contractions increased dramatically. Light was streaming into the dark bathroom from the open door. I was distantly aware that staff or other patients might see me, but I couldn't muster the energy to care. I had to continue my focus inward, had to attend to the pain and to muster strength the best I could. Nancy kept measuring my cervix, which meant I had to frequently lift my pelvis out of the water. Every movement hurt. Up to this point, I hadn't vocalized during contractions. I was so inwardly focused on getting through each one. What started off with a low groan turned into a full-fledged howl. I was on a rollercoaster of pain; up, down, all around me was pain. I tried to open my eyes, but they were so heavy.

One more contraction and I lost my breath and my pinpointed concentration. Suddenly I couldn't help myself. "When is the point of no return?" I managed to say. "Am I beyond having some drugs to help with the pain?"

"It's never too late, Colleen."

Damn it. I don't want this choice, I told myself. I wanted her to tell me it was too late so I wouldn't have to make the decision not to accept help from medication. But even in my near delirium I knew that life was all about making choices for oneself. I knew that a person never really gets to pawn her choices off on someone else. I had to decide *something*. The best I could do was to decide to wait until after the next contraction. I would have to go moment to moment on this.

Then, up the pain rollercoaster I went again. "Oh, I can't do this."

Did I really just say that? I asked myself. After everything I'd been through in my life, did I really, in the truest part of my heart, believe I could NOT do this?

No. Feeling I couldn't do this was just that: a feeling. And feelings come and go just like contractions. *Ride it out*, I told myself.

With the next contraction, something was different. Something was coming out of me. "Oh, what's happening?" I instinctively started to push. Was the baby coming?

"Oh don't worry, dear, just a little poop. I think you're body wants to push." No one had told me about this. I was embarrassed; mortified actually. I'd never pooped in front of my husband before. But I coached myself through it: *Embarrassment is just a feeling. Ride it out*. Nancy put on a clean plastic glove, and without hesitation, scooped my little turd from the tub and dropped it into the toilet behind her in one fell swoop. Clearly this wasn't new to her.

"Colleen, you need to change your breathing. Open your eyes, Colleen."

Nancy was right in front of me, her breath stale, and her first two fingers standing at attention in front of my face. "Okay, Colleen, you're not dilated enough to push yet, so I want you to pretend my fingers are a candle and you're trying to blow out the flame. Like this: *who, whoo, whooooo*."

I mimicked her breathing breath for breath. My body wanted to push so badly, it was nearly impossible to resist the urge. Nancy kept breathing with me, and I focused directly on her fingers, as if I were really blowing out a candle.

"Lift up your pelvis again, Colleen. Let's see how far along you are." I wanted this to stop. I just wanted it all to stop. *Ride it out.* I grabbed the sides of the tub, lifted my pelvis, and allowed Nancy to stick her fingers into my cervix. "Okay, let's go." She turned to Mark and the student midwife and said, "Help me get her out of the tub. We need to get you to bed to start pushing. Are you ready to have a baby?" The air instantly cooled as I heard her words, and I swore I could see sparkles all over the dark bathroom. *I'm going to have a baby.*

Once back in bed, pushing felt right, like what I was made to do. I could only lie on my back, so with every push, I brought my leg and stump up to my chest and gave it my all. This was a full-body experience; even the muscles behind my ears were involved. After nearly an hour of pushing, the persistent ache in my leg and nerve pain in my stump made it difficult to lift them to my chest on my own. Mark straddled me from behind, lifting my torso and bringing my stump up to my chest while the student midwife stood on my right maneuvering my leg. With each push, Nancy voiced her encouragement. "That was a good one!" "You're stretching nicely." "Oh, I see some hair." "Give me another one just like that." My leg pain was nearly unbearable. It felt made of glass, and each time the student lifted it to my chest, it felt like it was going to snap off at the hip. But I knew I wouldn't snap. *Ride it out,* I told myself. At the end of this there would be a baby. The contractions offered relief from my leg pain, not because the pain stopped, but simply because the contractions were more intense. I would take what relief I could get.

After three hours of pushing, I was weak. *Why isn't the baby coming out?* Then the thought occurred to me: *Is my child afraid to meet me—this crazy, depressed, angry mother who has cried her way through this pregnancy?*

Nancy told us she needed to call the doctor for an assessment. Panic cloaked my pain as I realized I might have to have a C-section. I didn't want seventeen hours of labor, three of which were pushing, to be in vain. Hearing Nancy in the background updating the doctor on the phone gave me renewed vigor. I gave each push everything I had, but I felt like I had during calisthenics day in elementary school when I heard the teacher say I was too slow to run the mile in ten minutes. I was trying as hard as I could, but I was falling short.

The doctor came half an hour later and decided to use a vacuum to suction the baby out. Mark, Nancy, and the student midwife all grabbed me confidently and turned by body ninety degrees so my leg was hanging off the side of the bed. Mark continued to straddle me from behind and be my muscles, moving my torso up and down as needed. I howled in pain as the doctor inserted the head of the vacuum into my swollen, tender vagina. I saw him look up at Nancy and say, "If the baby isn't out in three more pushes, we'll have to do a C-section." *Over my dead body*, I said in my heart. Up until now, I thought I had given each push my all, but upon hearing those words, I was filled with primal energy. I would not go into surgery. Mama Bear emerged, and I pushed from here to tomorrow. I pushed like I was birthing the world, and my baby came out on the third one.

A beautiful baby boy. Luke.

Nancy immediately placed my baby boy on my chest. I wept with joy and relief, instantly overcome with the purest love I'd ever known.

Once the midwives had cleaned me up, I lay on the bed with Luke and Mark. Luke looked up at me, big-eyed and quiet, and I was overwhelmed, humbled by his beauty, and completely in awe. I felt like I was looking into the eyes of God. *Are you one of the ones I erased all those years ago? Did you wait for me?*

Nancy noticed Luke fussing a bit and suggested I nurse him. I felt like a sixteen-year-old at her coming-of-age party, finally joining the ranks of all the other women in the world. For years, I'd watched family and friends breastfeed their children, wondering if I'd ever have that honor. Then there he was, suckling at my breast, a continued union of our bodies nurturing each other. In that moment, I had a visceral understanding that the struggle through my pregnancy was not in vain. The remaking of my identity would not be in vain. Luke was my gift to the world. And he was worth all of it.

We were discharged from the hospital the next day. Because of the long hours of pushing, my genitals were too swollen for me to wear my prosthetic leg. I sat in a wheelchair, just like when I left the hospital after the accident. Back then, however, I was filled with questions about why the hell my life was saved. This time, the answer was lying asleep in my lap.

Life was slow. Those first few weeks, as my body recovered, my mobility was very limited. I still wasn't able to wear my prosthetic leg, and I couldn't hop like I did in my pre-pregnancy days. Instead, I used a drafter's chair on wheels to get around the house. I spent most of my day in bed or on the couch, blissed out as I held or nursed Luke. I couldn't wait to change his diaper so I could marvel at his naked, whole body for a few minutes. I marveled at his two perfect little legs, his delicate fingers, his sweet earlobes. I looked back at my pregnancy and could see with the clarity that only comes in hindsight. I had focused on the part of my body that was missing as I was making this perfectly whole human being inside of me. And now I was focused on the perfect little body of that human being. My attention was where it should be.

Visitors streamed in and out to meet my son. Family came over for longer visits. My mom came over to help out periodically, and as predicted, she held Luke in her arms and called him the "sweetest heart of Jesus." I loved seeing my mother hold my child. Though her hands had aged, they were the same hands that held me in just the same way, the same hands that fumbled for my diaper pin, the same hands that gently swooped the warm, wet washcloth over my body as she gave me a bath. I saw her do all these things with Luke and developed a new appreciation for all she'd gone through over the years.

When my mom first saw me scooting around the house on the

drafter's chair, she gasped and brought her hand to her mouth. I saw the pain in her eyes. Just a year ago, I would have been offended or angry that she felt sadness and pity for me. But with a child of my own who I would kill for if anyone or anything wanted to hurt him, I could start to understand her violent need to protect me, even when I'd been quick to interpret her protection as judgment or expectation.

I saw pity in the eyes of other people as well when they visited and realized how much function I had lost. I didn't know if Mom or anyone else could understand that everything I'd given up was worth it. I was only at the precipice of understanding that my relationship with Luke would impact my life so much more than a kayak trip or a hike in the woods, but I sensed this truth. Those experiences put me in the presence of God. When I held Luke in my arms, I was holding a piece of God.

20

. ● .

DEEPER INTO DISABILITY

Few mothers experience constant bliss once the reality of taking care of a baby hits. As the weeks and months progressed, while I had many moments of holding Luke and feeling a deep connection to God, I was also still barely able to walk—and this impacted my ability to take care of him. I still couldn't get enough of Luke. There wasn't anything about him, not even his tongue, that wasn't absolutely perfect and beautiful to me, but I also couldn't get to him quickly when he needed me if he was in his crib and I was folding clothes in the other room. I couldn't carry him down the stairway to the basement where Mark and I watched TV.

In quiet moments, I marveled that this perfect little being came from my imperfect body. But sometimes my love wasn't enough. When Luke developed colic at three months, I wanted to comfort him as I'd comforted my nephew Brendon eleven years earlier, walking and bouncing him to help him calm down and to release the gas bubble that tormented him. But I was still managing life on my crappy pregnancy leg, and I couldn't balance for long periods with a squirming baby in my arms. I was at a total loss for what to do for him. And although a part of me understood that I was facing what every mother faces—the longing and incapacity to take away pain from her child—I also feared that I might be missing something more than my leg. What if I hadn't inherited the mommy gene?

I'd brought this baby into the world and now was powerless to help him.

My whole life I'd been a deep sleeper, so being up in the middle of the night was a challenge and lent itself to ruminations. One night, to foster calm for both Luke and me, I put on "Precious Little Angel" by Annie Lennox and held Luke in my arms, swaying to the beat of the music as I softly sang along. "Precious Little Angel, won't you spread your light on me. I was locked up in the darkness, now you've come to set me free . . ."

I rocked and sang and cried, still so amazed by the miracle of his life, remembering how hard my pregnancy had been. Now it was dawning on me that this body of mine was going to hamper my ability to care for my child. My lower back began to ache deeply, so I shifted Luke to my shoulder and bobbed up and down. This offered temporary relief for him but increased the pain in my stump. Luke was gaining weight quickly and was a big boy, close to thirteen pounds at three months.

A tear slipped down my face. As my frustration and urgency to calm him grew, I could feel another layer of the grief onion peeling away. All of Luke's life, I was going to bump up against limitations. My own pain was going to hamper my ability to soothe his. As Luke continued crying, I sat down on the sofa where I'd spent most of my pregnancy and pulled him off my shoulder so I could see his little distressed face. He was inconsolable and, to be honest, so was I. But by now I knew that speaking what was true for me often brought a bit of relief.

"Hey little buddy, I can't keep walking you around this living room. I'm at the end of my rope here and I'm sorry. I'll do the best I can for you, but tonight it looks like you and I will just have to sit here and cry it out together." And that's what we did.

Eventually, Luke's colic disappeared and we all slept a little better. I often carried Luke around in a sling, but I was afraid of myself, unsure of my ability to protect him, should I fall. And then as Luke grew, the sling became more and more uncomfortable for him. At five months, he protested when I tried to put him in it, so I held him in my arms instead, usually slung over my hip—the side without the amputation—completely oblivious to the damage I was doing. My lower back developed a deep ache and I began to feel sharp pains in my knee. It was time to replace my pregnancy leg with something more permanent and functional. Because I was nursing, my pregnancy weight was melting off, but I would never fit into my pre-pregnancy leg again because of the subtle changes in the position of my hips and pelvic area caused by the pregnancy.

I saw my prosthetist Kirk for weekly fittings and adjustments for a new and improved leg. Through each week of what was a two-month process I dared to become excited. *Once I have a regular leg again*, I thought, *I'll get back to normal.* I couldn't wait to rid myself of the uncomfortable waist belt of my pregnancy leg, to sit without discomfort, to walk without pain.

But of course, I should have known by now that adjustment to a new leg took time—time spent building up new calluses under new blisters. And it took time to adjust to a new gait, a new way of sitting on the toilet, a new way to balance holding my child in my arms.

The moment I put on the new leg, my stomach sank to the floor. It skewed my body, distorted my posture, and rubbed hard up in my crotch. I realized what I already knew: "normal" to me wasn't really normal to begin with. My normal is being an amputee.

I allowed myself some grumbling and self-pity as I drove home, made my way into the house, and found my place on the familiar sofa. Mark came to me with Luke in his arms. Luke stretched his body from Mark's, wanting me to hold him. I reached up and took him. Luke's deep dimples emerged as he broke into a smile, and his arms flapped with impatience. He reached down and lifted my shirt. After I rearranged my bra, he latched on and began to suck enthusiastically. I stroked his soft blond hair, and my self-pity melted into gratitude for my little family. I let out a heavy sigh. *He's worth it all.*

Mark sat down next to us and started rubbing my neck. "I'm sorry, Colleen. I know this is hard."

I was grateful for his kindness and selflessness.

"I just want be able to keep up. He'll be walking soon, you know? How can I be a good mother to him if I can't keep up?"

"You're an amazing mom, honey. Just give yourself a while to adjust to the new leg. It'll get better." My disability was mine, but Mark's loving presence made me feel less alone. As Luke nursed, I rested my head on Mark's shoulder, appreciating how patient he had been and how I was starting to trust that he truly was a partner. I kept waiting for him to hate me for being disabled. But it looked like he never would.

Luke started crawling at six months and walking at ten. I loved to watch him as he struggled with each movement. I could see the connections forming in his brain, the learning process in action. I wondered how jumbled my brain paths must be after learning subtle new ways to walk eight different times over the past nineteen years after each of my new legs was handed to me. Here I was again, right alongside Luke, relearning what my body should already know how to do. I walked up and down steps, one at a time, just like Luke. I caught myself teetering, finding my balance with the new leg, just as Luke found his.

Mark finally explored the park three blocks away from our house and started taking Luke to the swing set. One warm Saturday, Mark encouraged me to join them. "Why don't you come with us, honey? Last weekend, I put Luke in the baby swing and he just loved it. You gotta see him laugh when he's in that thing." A flash of fear swept through me as I tried to map out how far the park was. Could I walk there and back comfortably? Maybe not, but how could I say no to an invitation to see my child laugh while he was swinging? I put Luke in the stroller, and we started the three-block walk to the park. When we were nearly at the park I tripped on a crack in the sidewalk and lurched forward, pushing the stroller away from me. Mark casually ran up to grab the stroller, just a few feet ahead of us, while I stopped my momentum and stood still to catch my breath. The sudden physical movement of nearly falling triggered an emotional response. I stifled my tears. "I'm sorry, I didn't mean to . . ."

"Are you okay?" Mark put his arm on my elbow supportively.

"Yeah, I'm fine." I took a deep breath and kept walking. But I was filled with guilt and fear. What if Mark hadn't been there to intercept the stroller? How far from me might it have strayed before I would have been able to right myself and catch up with it? A terrifying worry was growing in me that I might not be able to protect Luke—that my lack of mobility would prevent him from having something very basic: safety. I was used to going through this process of learning to walk on a new leg alone, in private. I had always been able to manage my amputation, but only just—and only by myself. Now I needed to figure out how to manage my adjustment while staying present for my family and keeping my child safe. Could I do it?

Once we entered the park, we walked over a grassy lawn to the play area, which was nestled in a grove of fir trees. Sawdust chips layered the ground, forcing me to alter my gait to manage the uneven surface. We put Luke in the swing, gently pushed him, and laughed with him as he squealed in delight. In my spiritual quest, I was learning to stay present in the moment, to be in the here and now. And here with Mark and Luke, in all his innocence and purity, right now, all was well. I was able to let go of my negative feelings, if only for a few minutes, and stand on firm footing, filled with love and joy.

On our walk back, my stump started tiring and cramping, and a small raw spot developed from the incessant rubbing of my prosthetic leg against the delicate skin. The sore, though small, burned with a deep intensity. I exaggerated my limp more to try to avoid the rubbing, but that didn't help. I was walking slowly, and Mark slowed his pace to match mine. Luke was blowing spit bubbles in his stroller and playing with his rattle. I knew Mark didn't care how fast we walked, but I hated being the one to slow us down. I was a yo-yo. Up with the joy of love flowing to and from my family, and down with frustration as I constantly butted up against the reality of my body.

"We're fine walking with you. Don't worry about it." Mark seemed genuinely happy just to have the three of us out on a walk together.

I wished it could be enough for me that we were all together. It was so simple for Mark, and yet for me, achieving contentment was so difficult. It was my life's work, it seemed.

"Can I do anything to help?" he said quietly, sensing my discouragement.

"No. There's nothing you can do. This is my journey, Mark."

It was one thing for Mark to see my weakness. But the difficulty of this particular layer of grief for me was that I had to start giving the message that I had limitations to my son so early in his life. Whenever Luke became too heavy to hold, I would have to say, "I have to put you down, buddy, Mommy can't hold you anymore." How often would I have to expose my limits, my weakness, to my son? I hadn't been a mother for long, so I didn't yet realize that admitting our limitations and boundaries to our children is every parent's grief point. What was "missing" in my parenting might be more obvious than another parent's lack of empathy or poverty of spirit, but it wasn't any more or less dire. I just didn't know that yet. And I would have to learn it step by step, just as I'd had to learn everything else.

21

• ● •

FACING MY LIMITATIONS

My new leg finally became my new normal, and though I wasn't fit as I had once been, I was finally able to walk relatively pain free again. Taking a stroll to the park with Mark and Luke was always worth the effort. Luke sat in the toddler swing and squealed with delight as we pumped him higher and higher. Moments like these centered me. Watching Luke become a person fulfilled me beyond belief, and I soon moved through the resentment I'd felt during my pregnancy, when I'd feared I was losing my self-made identity. I'd had my twenties and early thirties to become myself, after all. Now it was his turn.

And while the joy of watching Luke grow was working a wondrous healing in many respects, it also made me aware that as he got older, his needs would become more complex. There was a haunting little voice that nagged at me, urged me to walk a little more, try a little harder, to get back a piece of the fitness I had lost during and since the nine months of pregnancy, as if fitness alone could make me all that my child would need me to be.

I tried. I really did. I even tried to reignite my passion for skiing by taking a trip up to Snoqualmie Pass with my friend from work, Alice, and her husband, Joe. But after my third run on the mountain, I ran out of steam and became completely exhausted. My joints weren't pliable anymore. My good leg wasn't strong as it used to be. When my outrigger broke in the early afternoon, I was thankful to have an excuse to sit in the lodge the rest of the day waiting for Alice and Joe to finish skiing. I didn't want to admit it, but my body would never again be what it had been before pregnancy. Growing a human being inside of me had done some permanent damage, and I was going to have to find a way to adapt to that.

As Luke moved through his early developmental stages, the impact of my disability became a stronger, more palpable part of my daily existence. For the first eighteen years of my life without a leg, I was mostly able to pick and choose the activities that would challenge me—like skiing. In fact, I put a lot of emotional energy into trying to control situations so I would be challenged just enough to be successful.

When I became pregnant and had no control over the physical hurdles, big or small, that came my way, I'd harbored hope that the limitations introduced during pregnancy wouldn't last after Luke was born; but I could see that they had. I was almost back to square one in terms of the speed at which I could move through the world. And as he started exploring his independence, I realized that my limitations could put Luke in danger. My fears started small but grew as he grew.

With a toddler, the risks I took note of were not like my risk-taking of yesteryear. They were subtle and profound. Instead of jumping out of an airplane with a parachute on my back, I learned to open my heart to the sadness I felt when I had to say, "No, honey, Mommy can't run with you. You run ahead, and I'll watch." And now the risks in my life had higher stakes because I was not the vulnerable one. Luke was.

I simply couldn't run after him. And if there is one thing the mother of a toddler needs to be able to do, it is to give chase.

When Luke first started walking, Mark and I took him to the beach on a warm September day. Mark held Luke in his arms as we made our way over the grass and down to the water. I wanted to carry him, but I didn't feel comfortable. I was afraid I would trip on the uneven ground and hurt him, unable to shield him from the fall and catch myself at the same time. The minute Luke saw the waves lapping at the shoreline, he wriggled out of Mark's arms and waddled as fast as his plump little legs could carry him. Mark and I were next to him as he walked over the dewy grass and onto the rocky beach. He masterfully navigated his way over the small rocks, all the way down to the water. I marveled at how his young brain and body could adapt so quickly to this terrain, while I struggled to maneuver over the pebbles.

Mark and I lingered a few steps behind as we laughed at how adorable he was as he toddled along. When Luke arrived at the water's edge, he didn't stop; he kept walking, unaware, toward the waves. "Luke, stop!" I half shouted, half laughed as Mark hurried over to scoop him up. Luke tried to wriggle out of Mark's arms, frustrated he couldn't grab a shiny rock he had his eye on. "Oh my God, he was going to walk right in the water, wasn't he?" I was shocked.

"I guess he was. Wow." Mark was as perplexed as I was. As new parents, we were discovering that children are not born with the instinct for self-preservation. Teaching that skill is the job of the parents. I found this simultaneously interesting and terrifying. If I had to teach my son the most basic common-sense rules, what happened if I forgot or neglected to teach him something before he encountered that situation? What if I failed? And what if Mark hadn't been there in that moment on the beach? Could I have reached him in time, before a crashing wave swamped him?

Reality hit home. And fear flooded in. How was I going to mother this precious soul if I couldn't keep up with him? An awesome terror filled my heart. How could I be all he needed me to be with only one leg? Slow. Limping. Often tired. I would try, but what if that wasn't enough?

I had to face the very real possibility that I might not be enough for the first time on a cold Tuesday just after the older children in our neighborhood had returned to school in early September. Luke was two and a half.

We had learned that he loved walking around the neighborhood searching for rocks and pebbles. A walk down the block could take fifteen minutes, so enamored was he with each stone he found. He'd pick it up with his chubby hand, eyes glistening, and hold the rock in the air, bursting with excitement. "Look, Mommy!" he'd squeal, as if it were the first rock ever discovered.

When we came to a crosswalk, I'd grab his hand in a vice grip and teach him how to look for cars. "Look right," I'd say in a singsongy voice that ended on a high note as I dramatically turned my head to the right. "Look left," I'd continue, with my singsongy voice now ending on a low note as I comically turned my head to the left. If I could teach my son anything, it would be to protect himself from getting hit by a car. Never a car. Our neighborhood didn't have a lot of traffic, but one could never be too careful.

This Tuesday while we were walking, as my mind wandered to my mental to-do list, Luke tired of the rocks. He spotted something across the street and down the block. Before I knew what was happening, he ran off the sidewalk, into the middle of the street, his plump arm extended, his index finger pointing. "Look, Mommy!" Giggles issued forth as he ran *right down the middle of the road*!

Fear gripped me as if a rabid dog was attacking my heart. He was so fast, and he was out of reach before I knew it. "Luke! Stop!" I screamed. Luke didn't stop. "Stop! Stop! Stop!" Luke kept running and laughing. Didn't he understand I couldn't run after him? Didn't he know what a car could do to him? He wasn't running *across* the street where he might reach safety on the other side; he kept running down the *middle* of the street.

As I hop-skipped after Luke, my best version of running, my eyes darted up and down the road. A car was a block away, coming toward us. "Luke! Stop!" I screamed, with high-pitched terror in my voice. Luke kept running down the street. I willed my body to go faster, right leg skipping, left leg following with a long hop. I had to reach out and grab him, but he was too fast for me, and too far away. He was now twenty-five feet in front of me, the farthest he'd ever been away from me alone in my presence. I was absolutely certain the car was going to hit him. I could see the whole scenario unfolding in my imagination, and my body contracted with the memory of the pain I'd experienced in my own accident. In my mind's eye, I watched my son die. My insides contorted at the thought; heat infused my body. The metallic taste in my saliva returned: the taste of trauma and loss.

I put my hand up in a "stop" position as I hop-skipped after Luke. The car didn't stop. I realized the person in the car probably couldn't see me, since they were still a block away. Luke was still running in the middle of the street, laughing as he turned his head to see if I was catching up with him. *No, don't look behind you—keep looking ahead so you don't trip!* He neared the edge of the street and then inexplicably slowed down. I finally made headway and caught up to him, trembling with panic and adrenaline. I scooped him up into my arms and pressed him to me.

"*Ow*, Mommy, hurts."

"I'm sorry, buddy," I heaved, half sobbing. I nuzzled my face into his neck and took a long whiff of him: baby skin and sunshine, warm earth and Cheerios. "Luke," I said firmly, "don't ever run into the *street*. That's dangerous. We *walk* . . . we walk on the *sidewalks*. Do you understand me?" He was only two and a half, but I wanted to will him to understand how important this was. And yet I didn't want to scare him—didn't want him to have the same taste of iron in his mouth that I had in mine.

Luke squirmed his way out of my arms, slid down my torso, and reached the ground. He turned around and showed me what he was running after: a broken piece of a red Mylar balloon caught in a bush. My son almost died for a broken balloon.

The counseling I'd done before Mark and I became involved helped me deal with many of my fears, but nothing had prepared me for the terror of watching my son run down the center of the street. There I was on the sidewalk with Luke, catching my breath, resisting the internal trembling, and wiping the tears from my check before Luke could see them.

I wasn't bereft simply because the possibility existed that my son could disappear from my life via death by car or any other horrible disaster; I was devastated that I lived in a body that I couldn't count on to save him.

22

• ● •

FINDING MY NORMAL

Luke was two when he realized his mommy was different than other mommies. One day after a shower, before I put on my leg, I sat on my big bed with Luke. He crawled over to me, and I started to tickle him. His unvarnished giggles filled the room like a chorus of singing angels. I started to move my naked stump around, curious about how he might react. Since my leg was cut off right above the knee, I have a long stump. I'd often felt that it must look creepy to other people, but Luke just rolled over and exclaimed, "Mommy baby leg."

I'd always hated referring to my residual limb as a "stump." The word conjured images in my mind of trees being violently hacked down, my leg being whacked off. I liked the term "baby leg."

I wanted to help Luke understand my disability, so I hopped into his room and grabbed the doll my brother's family gave me a few days after Luke was born. When I'd opened their gift and saw a doll with a prosthetic leg, tears welled in my eyes. I was so grateful Luke had a doll that normalized his mommy's body. I brought her to the bed now and took off her little plastic prosthetic leg. Luke pointed to the doll's stump and said, "Baby leg!"

"That's right. She has a baby leg just like I do." That's the term I would use from now on.

Changing the name of my residual limb didn't bring back the function I had lost, but it did invite me to think about the new definition for myself that was starting to unfold before my eyes. *I am a disabled mother.* I had to figure out how to function as a disabled mother. I didn't know another amputee mother. I didn't know any disabled mothers. Ever since I'd lost my leg, I'd dealt with my amputation for my own sake, but now it was up to me to figure out how to manage the impact of it on Luke.

As had been the case for so many years, grief would be my teacher.

I'd stopped working one year after Luke was born and, after many months of spending my days solely with Luke, loneliness crept up on me. So just before Luke had his second birthday, I found a Mommy and Me toddler group for us to join, hoping we could both make some new friends.

Our first day of Mommy and Me was a warm September morning. I packed Luke up and drove to the playground, anxious about joining a group of women who already knew one another, but determined to widen our lives outside of our small home. On the north end of the playground was a building that functioned as a community center and was used for meetings and other gatherings. I made my way to the entrance and checked in with Lucy, the group facilitator who I'd talked to on the phone the previous week. I shuffled farther into the room, a wide-open space filled with children's play things, and stood on the sidelines of the group of ten women, who were all chatting with one another. One woman finally opened the circle to me just a bit, and I tried to find a way into the conversation. Luke tentatively joined some boys who were playing with big blocks and quietly looked at them with the same uncertainty I felt.

At ten sharp Lucy rang a bell and announced in a singsongy voice, "It's Circle Time, boys and girls. Come to the rug, please." All the other moms found their children and scampered to a round colorful rug in the middle of the room and sat around the edges, echoing its shape. *Oh great*, I internally moaned, *I have to sit on the floor.*

There is always a moment in every group when my prosthetic leg gives itself away. Sitting on the floor would accomplish this for sure. Regardless of how relaxed the rest of my body is, my prosthetic leg sticks straight out like a rifle. Made of plastic and wood, the foot stays at a ninety-degree angle, even when my body is in repose. Whereas most moms sat "crisscross applesauce" with their child tucked neatly in their lap, I sat down with my left leg sticking out into the middle of the circle, and bent my other leg at the knee.

It was always hard for Luke to get comfortable in my lap when I sat on the floor. Because my prosthetic leg reached all the way to my hip, half of his "seat" was as hard as a rock. He settled in the best he could and gave me a smile. I noticed some of the other moms look curiously from the corners of their eyes and then quickly look away. A few children noticed the metal at my ankle sticking out the end of my pants, too, but without the reserve of the adults. One mom noticed her child was staring and tried to casually redirect her child's attention. I shifted a bit to get comfortable and avoided catching the eye of anyone around the room.

Lucy, who looked to be in her fifties and who oozed warmth and comfort, welcomed us all to the group. "And we'd like to welcome new members Colleen and Luke into the group today. Thank you for coming." The other moms around the circle nodded their welcomes.

Lucy led us in singing a child's song about an elephant stomping around in the clover. The moms, smiles spread across their faces, sang along enthusiastically, looking at their children with raised eyebrows, an invitation to sing along. The children started singing, some quietly, others with equal enthusiasm. The tune was catchy and the words repetitive, so I tentatively sang along. Luke was more reticent and stuck to observing.

We sang about five more songs that first day, many which required hand gestures. I felt silly and self-conscious and marveled at the other moms' unabashed participation. After song time, while Lucy and a few moms fixed a light snack, the rest of us followed the children outside to the play area. This was our chance to mingle and chat informally.

Over the course of the next month, women began approaching me more, and I them. We easily chatted about the ups and downs of mothering our toddlers. Some of the women had older children, and I tucked away their tips about the inevitable phases Luke would be entering.

Though I could talk about general parenting issues, I couldn't talk to the other moms about how disabled I felt, about the loss of function I'd endured over the last few years. Experience had taught me people didn't want to hear about the downside to being an amputee. Over the years, most new people in my life seemed to want only to see me mount the odds or, at the very least, look and act normal. So I tried to act normal with my new acquaintances, even though I didn't feel it. I felt protective of my story, of my true self. I lived in secret terror that others would discover how truly disabled I was and think I shouldn't have become a parent in the first place, so I dropped references about having skied, backpacked, or kayaked to prove I could be active.

While I could compare to any other mom on an emotional and intellectual level, on the playground my physical limitations became more pronounced. I couldn't run around with Luke. I watched wistfully as other moms played a game of chase with their children. My heart broke every time I thought about how I couldn't share the joy of running with my little boy. Even wrestling with him was a challenge because my prosthetic leg could hurt him.

Luke had already distinguished himself as an "observer" in life. He didn't sing the circle songs until he had watched and learned them first. He looked at how the other boys adeptly ran around on the jungle gym before climbing, so I knew he was aware, on some level, of my difference, but he never indicated it bothered him. He treated me the same way all the other toddlers treated their moms: clinging when he was scared or tentative, and running away to play when he felt safe.

On the second visit to the Mommy and Me playgroup, when it was time to go outside and watch the kids swarm the play structure, I watched as Luke climbed and scrambled and I found it impossible to have a casual conversation with the mom standing next to me. I couldn't focus on what she was saying. Fear for Luke's safety gripped my heart. My pulse quickened and my breath started to come in shallow bursts. I excused myself from the other woman and sidled up to Luke just to be near him. I dubbed myself his "spotter."

As he grabbed hold of the rung above him on the climbing cage, my sweat glands began working overtime. I quickly grew wet around my neck and under my arms. Why weren't the other mothers over here with me spotting their children? Everyone needed a spotter, didn't they? Especially if you were going to hang from a high bar or swing wildly across monkey bars that were just barely in reach? Especially if you were going to climb *on top* of the tube covering the slide?

By the time Luke and I got into the car to go home, I felt worn and old, like I could go to bed and sleep for a million years. After I got Luke in his car seat, I sat behind the wheel for a few moments and put my hand on my heart. I could feel it pounding. I'd intended to go to the grocery store when we left playgroup, but I was done for the day.

Each week required a true force of commitment in order for me to return and keep vigil over the playground. Each week I stood in front of the mirror at home before leaving for Mommy and Me and saw how I was not like the other moms. None of them talked about the fear I felt. I did not see terror in their eyes that I suspected they must see in mine.

One day, after we'd been attending the group for about two months, I was standing near the tube slide with a few of the moms when I saw a group of children gathered at the bottom, gently pushing one another to get to the opening. They were too little to see that at the top of the slide there was another group of children, Luke included, vying to be the next one to go down the slide.

One woman was talking about using time-outs to teach kids patience. "So I was reading an article in *Mothering* magazine about . . ." I couldn't listen. Panic was rising in my chest as I imagined a child at the bottom of the slide getting a face full of shoes when the next child slid down. I quickly scurried over to monitor the slide activity.

"Hey, kids," I said as I corralled the children at the bottom of the slide away from the opening "Why don't you go up to the top and slide down. We slide *down* the slide."

"No, I want to climb up and then slide down," one of the girls said excitedly.

"But there are other kids at the top already coming down, so you could get hurt," I tried to explain. I looked over to the group of moms engrossed in their conversation. They continued talking, unconcerned. Was I overreacting? I looked down momentarily and saw that my hands were trembling. I had to get the children to move. I decided I'd try to entice them up the stairs to the top of the slide with a contest. "Hey, look at this dinosaur head up here. Who can touch it first?" That did it; they all scampered up the stairs, vying to be the first, and my chest opened up again.

I just couldn't stand how fraught this playground was with danger.

For the rest of that hour, I tried to hold my tongue and stand back, but when Luke grabbed the bar at the top of the slide and swung like a gorilla before plopping his butt onto the slide, I practically had a heart attack. An image of him falling and breaking his back came to me. I played out the whole scene in my mind: me running up to him and realizing he was badly injured. Luke reaching up for me in utter pain. Me yelling to a mom to call an ambulance. Luke crying and begging me to take the pain away. Me riding in the ambulance with Luke and calling Mark when we arrived at the hospital. Luke ending up in a wheelchair for the rest of his life.

Luke got up off the slide and raced to the swings.

"Luke, NO, honey. *No* swinging. You might get hurt." My words caught in my throat. I turned to the women standing next to me and said, "I think I'm coming down with a cold. I'd better get home before I give it to all of you." It was a lie. But I had to get off that playground.

Of course I understood Luke might get hurt. We all might get hurt. If anyone knew that, I did. But I had never felt this kind of abject, paralyzing fear before: the fear of my child's imminent death. What did Luke hear in my voice when I forbad him to swing? What was I passing on to him when I hovered beside him at the slide? I didn't want him infected by my dysfunction and yet I didn't know how to stop it from happening.

I still saw my therapist Lynn occasionally when I bumped up against myself and faced peeling away another layer of the trauma that had informed my life. I planned to talk to her about my playground anxiety eventually, and then something happened one night that made me get serious about figuring out how to work with my increasing fear.

I was folding clothes on the couch. Luke was sitting in his chair eating Cheerios and drinking juice. In a flash, the way these things happen, he accidentally spilled his juice—just knocked it right off the table onto the floor.

Panic and rage flooded me so quickly I couldn't catch myself. "Luke! That's not okay!" I screamed, rushing over from the couch where I was folding laundry. And then under my breath, "Goddamn it!" I hurried over to the counter to grab paper towels, ripping them off with urgency, as if something—what, I didn't know—depended on everything happening quickly. I rushed over to the table and cleaned up the spill with a vengeance, movements big and rough.

"I didn't mean to," he whined as he backed away from me, his eyes cast down, tears welling. His tears brought me back to myself. What in the world was happening to me? I moved over to him and gave him a big hug, fully aware how contradictory this must feel to him. Once minute I'm yelling, the next I'm hugging.

"Luke, it's okay. I'm sorry I yelled. I know yelling hurts your heart. I'm so sorry." This wasn't the first time this had happened or only the second. I heard myself say those words too many times, but that night I wasn't just in the moment, I was also observing myself.

I was so focused on preventing an accident, I didn't know how to deal with this latent, frantic anxiety that lay just below the surface, nor did I truly understand its source. What I didn't understand was why anything unexpected, any disruption, flooded me. What I did know was that in my attempt to manage the possibility that catastrophe was right around the corner, I had wound myself up so tight that Luke was probably starting to feel that *he* was the problem.

I couldn't let this go on. I was hurting the very person I was trying to protect.

I made an appointment with Lynn as early as she could get me in after the juice incident. Sitting in her office, the walls lined with books, I asked her, "How can get rid of this hair-trigger panic and anger? I don't even like myself anymore."

Lynn probed. "What do you get anxious and mad about?" Even while giving examples of Luke's and Mark's minor transgressions and of the playground fiascos, I knew there was something deeper. Lynn had heard enough of my story by this point in our relationship and asked, "Can I tell you what I think?"

"Please." It would be a load off my shoulders to feel I had an ally.

"I think you were expected to perform, literally and figuratively, too soon after your accident. Tell me, how did you feel standing on your high school stage three months after losing your leg?"

"Honestly, I was a jumbled mess of emotions, from excitement to anger."

Lynn and I further explored the impact acting in the play had on me, as well as everything else that had happened so quickly after the accident, and how those experiences didn't allow me to integrate the trauma into my brain—or my heart. I already knew this was true, but I was finally ready to loosen the armor surrounding my heart.

"You can't deal with your children's humanity if you can't deal with your own. Tell me, do you want to bring your children into this trauma or do you want them to live their own lives?"

"Well, of course I want them to live their own lives. I don't want my trauma to be my legacy. But how? How do I let it go?"

"The first step is allowing yourself to *be* sad, to learn to live in and with your sadness. Though you've cried a lot, you constantly fight against being sad, like it's something you can get out of you and then be done with for good. Colleen, I think you're very sad." She paused, looked down at her lap, and then looked up at me.

I felt suddenly naked. And tears filled my eyes. She was right. That was the big and small of every struggle I'd had over the past twenty years. I was sad. Somehow I'd gotten into my head that sadness equaled weakness. Sadness is one of those emotions that thrusts us into vulnerability, like being a freshly molted crab floating in the sea waiting for her fresh shell to harden. And for me being vulnerable was as good as standing out on that freeway again trying to flag down some help. When I was angry, I tricked myself into believing that I wasn't exposed and didn't need protection. When I was angry, at least I was in charge of something.

"What would happen, Colleen, if instead of leaving your sadness at the door, you invited your sadness to dinner? Make a place for sadness at your table."

Well that's a silly idea, I thought. And then I remembered an evening when I was five years old. I had invited Indian Joe, the imaginary friend I played with out in the backyard, to dinner. Indian Joe knew some of the Native Americans who had felled the large trees in our yard many years ago. He was a kind, gentle, and sad man. Mostly we walked around the yard holding hands and talking. I didn't know why he was so sad, but I wanted to help him.

Indian Joe agreed to join us for dinner. When we walked inside, Mom was finishing the meal preparations and my older sister, Maureen, had set the table. I went to the silverware drawer and pulled out another setting and, since I couldn't reach, I asked

Maureen to reach into the cupboard for another plate. I took all of this to the table, pushed the plates and silverware over to squeeze in one more place setting. I went into the family room and dragged a chair to the kitchen table. Mom walked over to me, crouched down on her knees and asked, "Colleen, what are you doing?"

"I asked Indian Joe if he wanted to come to dinner. I'm setting him a place."

"So he said yes?" she prodded.

I nodded. "I want him to sit next to me."

"Okay, sounds good, honey." Mom stood up and started bringing the dishes of food to the table.

I spent a lot of time with Indian Joe, and I desperately wanted for him to be real. Mom's acceptance of him joining us for dinner made me believe that perhaps he was.

After we'd said our prayers, I put a piece of Shake 'n' Bake chicken on his plate and some iceberg lettuce salad. He smiled at me and said, "Thank you." While the rest of the family chattered around the table, Indian Joe and I sat there quietly and I helped him eat his dinner.

Though Indian Joe left my life a few months after that, his presence had been real and made an impact. A scorning word or a sarcastic attack from anyone in my family about his existence could have quickly killed him off, but their acceptance of him gave that relationship strength and allowed me to keep him with me until I'd made it through that particular developmental stage.

I realized that I did know how to sit with my unseen companion, sadness. I was finally ready to have my new family welcome another member.

"What do you think, Colleen? Can you invite sadness to the table?"

"Yes. I can."

Lynn had given me permission to just be sad. Sad was normal. And I needed normalcy—true normalcy, more than anything. I'd been striving for it for years. That night at dinner I felt a little silly, but I went ahead and added another place setting to the table, just as I had as a little girl. Luke was oblivious. Mark cocked his eyebrow and asked, "Is someone coming for dinner?"

"I know this is a little 'out there,' but I set a place at the table for my sadness. I'm inviting sadness into my life without apology or shame, and this is my way of being intentional about that."

"Well, okay, then. Welcome, sadness!" Mark said and gave me a quick peck on the cheek as we brought the food to the table. I suspected he was as grateful for the chance to blatantly acknowledge my grief as I was.

I wasn't born a good mother, I was becoming one. As Luke grew, so did I. Though I'd tried to pass as normal since the accident, I had always focused on appearing to be normal on the physical level. I was learning that normalcy wasn't experienced on the outside as much as it was an internal experience. So, as Luke learned how to swing from the bars at the playground, I brought normalcy to his childlike moments by not catastrophizing his every move. As I was teaching Luke the safe limits of crossing the street, I was learning to accept my own limits; I couldn't protect him from everything. As I wiped his tears of sadness over his small losses, I vowed to never "shush" him, to never give him the message that his sadness was a burden for me. And I learned how to mother him from love and not from fear, because I was also learning how to mother the part of me that was still lying on the freeway.

We were both learning how to be *normal* human beings.

23

• ● •

SETTING BOUNDARIES

As I slowly made peace with both my strengths and my limitations as a mother, I also gradually became ready to learn how to create healthy boundaries between myself and the world around me. Again, my sweet son would help me learn what I needed to know.

In the summer when Luke was a toddler, I'd put on our bathing suits and my peg leg, the leg I use in the water, and take us to one of Seattle's parks to play in the wading pool. After spreading out our blanket, I'd get out the sunblock and slather his plump little body with lotion. Resisting like a greased pig, he'd try to squirm away, his eyes on the wading pool.

The first time we went, just as I knew would happen, I felt their eyes prickling my back. As Luke and I made our way across the grass to the pool, their whispers tickled my ears. I fully expected the looks and the whispers. What I didn't expect was that eventually they would begin to emerge, like the munchkins rising from the plants in the Land of Oz, to peer closely at my leg. Just like Dorothy, I was seen as unusual. Children didn't often see someone like me. My peg leg, attached to an otherwise normal-looking mom, made me unique. I looked like half suburban mother, half pirate. I walked with the stiff-legged swagger of Captain Ahab. And they couldn't resist.

"Go ahead and ask her," I heard one mother whisper to her child.

The little girl, along with some other children, approached me. Some of them were tentative; others came forward with unabashed confidence. But by the time I reached the pool and stepped into the water, there were about six children surrounding Luke and me. Standing in the middle of the wading pool, they peppered me with questions, and each seemed to mirror the personality of the child.

"Eeww, what happened?" asked a cute little girl in a tone of disgust. *God, I hate feeling judged by a child*, I thought as I composed my answer in my mind.

"I was in a car accident, and my leg got banged up, so the doctors had to take it off," I replied in a gentle voice.

"Did the car go crash?" asked a grungy little boy who was probably reluctant to leave his tractor in the dirt pile when his mom had called him in to get ready to go to the park.

"Yes, the car went crash."

"Was there a whole lot of blood?" asked a more timid child, who actually seemed concerned.

"Yes, there was blood, but the doctors made the bleeding stop."

"Did it hurt?" another wondered.

"Yes, it hurt, but I'm okay now. It was a long time ago."

"Did you cry?" This from a little boy who was probably trying to gauge how bad it was. If I cried, it was bad.

"Yes, I cried."

And then a brave child ventured, "Can I touch it?"

Before I could think, I said, "Sure. See, it's hard because it's made of plastic. I can't even feel you touching me."

After the children took turns touching my leg, squealing as if they'd just gotten away with something sneaky, they slowly dispersed. A few lingered, assuming Luke and I would play with them. I didn't want to hurt their feelings by ignoring them, so I half-heartedly attempted to engage with them. Luke tugged on my hand and looked up at me with pleading eyes. I took him to the park because I wanted him to be the center of my universe. Instead, and without inviting it, I had become the center of all these children's universes for a few minutes. I looked at his face and felt like I had failed him.

As we drove home that afternoon, I realized that Luke had just heard the story of how I'd lost my leg for the first time. I'd had fantasies of telling him this story when he was older—in some very intentional way that would help him understand without making him feel scared. But I hadn't known how to fend off the children at the park without hurting their feelings, so the story had spilled out. And now there it was.

There it was over and over again that summer, too. The same scene repeated itself every time Luke and I went to the wading pool. I felt the same discomfort every time. And every time, I looked at Luke's face afterward and wished I had a way to tell the other children to go away.

On a hot day late that summer, as we were getting ready to go to the wading pool, Luke asked, "Mommy, can you stop talking about your leg at the park?" His request said it all. It told me he was tired of hearing the same questions and the same answers. He was tired of his mommy being singled out at the playground. He was tired of my divided attention.

I knew I was tired of the questions, too, but I didn't know how else to handle them besides to answer. I tried to think back to my prying curiosity in my younger years with Linda, Becky, Rashid, and Gary—how I had wanted to know their stories so badly. They had kept their boundaries with me, had decided for themselves what they would and wouldn't talk about. But I couldn't remember how they'd done it. I only remembered my longing to find compatriots in my pain and the embarrassment I felt when I pried too deeply.

I couldn't count on the children at the park to figure out that they were out of line. I'd need to learn how to draw boundaries for myself—and for Luke.

Later in the week, sitting across from Lynn in her office, I posed the question to her, "*Can* I stop answering the children's questions?"

I saw the familiar twinkle in her eye when she knew we were onto something big. I still wanted an easy way out of uncomfortable situations, even after all this time of learning that life was often an uphill climb, but those eyes told me this one would require me to stretch my comfort zone.

"Why *do* you answer their questions?" she posed.

"Why? Because they ask."

"Yes, but why do *you* answer?"

I paused to consider. *Why did I answer them?* Then it hit me. "Because I feel responsible to these children. I want to relieve their fear of people who look different. I want to prove to them I'm normal and not a freak."

As we talked more, I remembered my youthful disgust of the boy in my high school choir class who had a deformed arm. I recalled my visceral fears and sick feelings about him and other people with missing body parts. Before my accident, a body with a missing part made me want to throw up. I didn't want people to feel that way about *me*. So telling the story of my accident made me a real person, a victim who had no choice about what her body looked like, and not just some disgusting freak. I was still fighting my own disgust by trying to prevent others from feeling it about me.

And then Lynn said something that blew my mind.

"You know, you don't have to answer their questions. You don't have to take care of them or make them comfortable." She went so far as to say, "It's the children's parents' job to tell their children what happened and to help them manage their feelings."

I considered this. "Well, I don't want the parents coming up to me and asking all their questions." That would be worse.

She suppressed a laugh. "No, they probably won't. You just tell the kids to go ask their parents what happened."

Whatever she was getting at still wasn't sinking in. "But they don't *know* what happened."

She nodded, seeing I was struggling. "True. But all they need to know is that you lost your leg and you wear a prosthetic leg to compensate. That's *all* the children need to know. And you don't have to be the one to tell them that."

Finally, a realization was coming over me like warm water in a shower. "You mean, I don't need to be responsible for all these children?" *Wow.* I thought. Was she giving me permission to let other people deal with their own curiosity and feelings about my missing limb?

"Do adults ask questions about your leg, too?" She peered over her glasses.

"Yes, a lot."

"Do you answer them?"

"Well, yes. I don't want to be rude. I want to be nice."

I had spent the last twenty years answering every single tactless question about my accident to avoid being rude to people. People didn't seem to realize their questions, especially the persistent questions that dug deeper into the specifics of the accident, forced me to open up my precious little cargo bin of memories. Having been conscious during the entire accident, except for the one fraction of a second when my leg was severed, my memory of losing my leg was crystal clear. If I knew anything, I knew I couldn't dwell on those memories for long without moving into a trauma response. At least once a week over the last twenty years some stranger asked me to recount that day. I could never talk about the accident without a little lump swelling up in my throat. And yet I couldn't be rude, could I? So I perfected a glib attitude and a wave of my hand to dismiss how sad it was. I walked away from those brief encounters with strangers feeling my glibness was a betrayal of my tender self. I then had to put those memories back in the cargo bin and stuff them under the bed of my heart after each encounter.

Lynn pointed out how ludicrous adults' questions were by giving me an alternative reply: "I'll tell you all about the worst day of my life if you tell me about the worst day of yours."

That stopped me dead in my tracks. My first reaction was complete resistance—there was no way I could say that to anyone. I pictured myself answering people's questions with her provocative answer instead of engaging in a five-minute conversation with them and I started to giggle nervously.

Maybe I could do it. Maybe I could really set this limit and claim my boundary. The pit of fear in my stomach told me it wouldn't feel natural to talk to people that way, but the relief and freedom I felt just thinking about the possible results made it clear that some kind of boundary had to be my next step. I left my session with a promise to Lynn and to myself that I would practice a handful of phrases I could use to set boundaries. I was determined to protect both myself and Luke from other people's sometimes well-meaning, but often detrimental, curiosity.

When I decided I wasn't going to answer any more questions, I felt big and powerful and small and scared all at the same time. While doing the dishes or folding the laundry, I practiced my responses for both children and adults.

"I'm here at the playground to play with my son. I'm sure your mom or dad can explain."

"I'll tell you about the worst day of my life if you tell me about the worst day of yours."

I finally understood that the children didn't need the gory details. Their own parents knew how much information to give and what language to use with their child far better than I did. I felt like my cells rearranged themselves in the course of one week once I adopted this new persona. There was a seismic shift in my attitude, in my understanding, about where my boundaries lay.

On the next hot day, I donned my shorts and took Luke to the park, ready to take the kids on. *Come on, let me have it. Give me your best shot. I can handle even the most insensitive, asinine question.*

We walked into the park, laid out our blanket, and applied the sunblock just like always. I glanced around me at the other park patrons. Not one whisper. We played in the wading pool. No one came up to us. We walked over to the playground. No one asked a single question. There were a few stares, which was normal and expected, but not one question. I was disappointed until I realized I'd gotten what I asked for: a peaceful trip to the park with my son. Was this a fluke or was I giving off different energy with my new resolve?

But a few weeks later, I would get to use these new boundaries. Mark and I took Luke to a park together on a Saturday. We were spinning on the roundabout when a boy about five years old ran up to us. "Hey, what's that?" he asked, pointing at my leg.

"I'm at the park with my son right now. You can talk to your parents about it." I scanned the park, but saw no other adults present. *Is this boy here alone?*

"They're not here. Hey, what IS that thing?" He walked over to me as the roundabout slowed down. I saw his hand reaching out to touch my leg. I could see this child was going to make me work at it.

I got up and walked a few feet away. "I'm playing with my son right now. Here, I'll spin," I said, turning my attention to my family. And I began spinning the roundabout.

"Is that real? Hey, what happened?" I gave Mark a desperate look. This was the kind of child who might go on relentlessly, each question inspiring a new one. I didn't want to jump on that merry-go-round, but I'd only practiced a few phrases.

Mark chimed in, direct and clear, "Stop asking questions."

My shoulders relaxed and I breathed. *Oh, so that's how to do it.* The boy, realizing I wasn't going to bite, didn't leave, but started talking about his new bike. I heard his dad, hailing him from across the park, to come home. We spent the next half hour playing peacefully, just the three of us.

If I were on a plane falling from the sky and all the air masks dropped from the overhead compartments, I wouldn't first help everyone else to get their mask on, put on my own, and then finally put on my son's. If I responded this way, he would be dead by the time I got to him. I realized that every time I answered someone's questions, I'd been taking care of that person first, then taking care of my need to take care of them, and I'd been leaving Luke out in the cold. This wasn't just a lesson in how to set my own boundaries; I found a deeper understanding of what it meant for me to be a mother.

My son comes first.

24

• ● •

ONE MORE TIME

My dream of having a noisy, swirling house full of six kids was long gone. I knew my body couldn't take six pregnancies, but I also couldn't fathom having only one child. It was soon time to think of giving Luke a sibling.

The parenting books I read cited over and over that the perfect age span between siblings is three years. While that factored into our decision about when to have another baby, the bigger and more compelling reason was that I was thirty-eight. Time was ticking. I understood I would lose some of my physical abilities during the pregnancy that would complicate life for both Luke and me, but I didn't have all the time in the world. If I was going to have another baby, it was now or never.

I felt emotionally ready. Since Luke's arrival in our lives I had grown so much. Of course I feared falling into depression again, but I had truly dealt with the identity issues that had brought me crashing down in first pregnancy, so I had some hope I could stave it off.

I realized something had completely changed for me in how I thought of myself one hot summer day in June just after I got pregnant. I was getting ready to go to a friend's retirement party. There were going to be people there I didn't know. The party was scheduled to start at five o'clock in the evening, which, in Seattle, meant the party would start off hot and quickly turn cool when the sun went down at about nine o'clock. If I wore shorts, I'd undoubtedly be asked "the questions," and have to fend them off with my new well-practiced boundary statements. If I wore pants, I'd be too warm for the first couple of hours.

I stood in front of my closet pondering what to do. A year ago, I would have worn the shorts, not only because of the weather, but also because the loss of my leg was so much of who I was and how I identified myself to strangers. It was my one special and unique quality. Although I'd always hated the looks and questions showing my leg invited, I'd appreciated that people would think highly of me when they saw my leg and learned I was so *able* to do so many things on my own. "Oh, she's so brave, such a survivor, how admirable," were whispers I didn't mind overhearing. Such sentiments helped me identify myself as strong and extraordinary, when deep inside I felt weak and irrelevant.

Ironically, other people's admiration also identified me as *disabled* since my success "in spite" of my disability is what they were commenting on. I'd lived in this quagmire of conflicting needs (to want people to leave me alone while also needing them to recognize and validate me) for too many years.

That night, while I was trying to decide what to wear, I realized I wanted to be recognized just for being me. On my own, I was enough to be liked. Naturally, I still questioned whether I had enough substance, enough humor, and enough interesting qualities to hold my own without my leg as a conversation piece. But the other irony was that just as I had accepted my limitations over the past three years of being a mother, I had also been through a process of letting go of identifying myself solely as an amputee.

I wore the pants—not to be secretive, not to avoid the questions per se, but to stand on my own two feet. I didn't *need* to be disabled in order to matter. What I'd discovered was that the totality of who I am far outweighs the part of me that's missing. I neither had to be Super Amputee, nor Poor Colleen. I was disabled, yes, but not unable. I was everything all once: strong and weak, happy and sad, extraordinary and limited in some ways. Just like everyone else.

For my second pregnancy, my prosthetist Kirk and I decided I should use my peg leg instead of the belted leg I used during my first pregnancy. He agreed to enlarge the socket as needed to accommodate my increasingly large "baby leg." The downside to using the peg leg was that I would spend my pregnancy (and probably nine months after my baby's birth as I lost my baby weight) walking stiff-legged like a pirate. The plus side was that wearing a leg with a suction socket versus one held on by a belt was infinitely easier and, I would come to find out, meant I wouldn't need to rely on crutches the last few months of the pregnancy.

Experience is a wise teacher. I approached the second pregnancy with an intimate understanding of the fetus's development and my limited body's potential deterioration. During my first pregnancy, the baby felt like an invader, ruining my life. I'd been miserable and then had worried about how each of my decisions and moods affected Luke. He turned out fine, despite the milkshakes, donuts, and weepy days. This second time around I was much more relaxed about what I was doing and what was happening to my body. Even as my body continued to remind me of its imperfections and constraints, I kept an even keel.

When I was six months pregnant, I started taking Luke to swim lessons at the YMCA twice a week. Being in the water was as good for me as it was fun for Luke. The water displaced the weight of the baby inside me and allowed me to easily maneuver my body. I held Luke's chubby, soft body in my hands, facedown so he could practice blowing bubbles and kicking. I threw him in the air and caught him as he hit the water. Our belly laughs echoed around the pool.

One day, after we had showered and changed, we were walking down the hallway to the car. I carried our tote bag, and Luke carried his pool toy. Suddenly, without any warning that might have allowed me to brace myself, I crash-landed on the floor. Luke stood beside me helpless as I lay catawampus on the ground. Pain registered in my hip and in the palms of my hands, which I'd instinctively used to try and catch myself on the way down. I slowly straightened myself out and sat up. Our toiletries and wet towels were scattered across the floor. At once I thought of the baby. My hands immediately rushed to my stomach. *Is the baby okay?* Tears sprang to my eyes. What just happened? Why had I fallen? I looked down and saw that the metal rod, the bottom half of my peg leg, had broken off from the socket—the metal connection at the bottom of the socket had been worn thin and had simply snapped. Scanning the hallway, I saw the metal rod ten feet away from us across the floor. I looked at Luke, worried he'd be scared. Once he saw I was okay, he'd begun playing with his pool toy.

Everything was all right. I wasn't hurt. Luke was calm. The baby was fine.

"Luke, help Mommy gather our things," I said calmly.

"Okay, Mommy. What happened?"

"My leg broke, honey. I need to get some help."

"Are we going home?" he asked.

"Yeah, buddy, once I find someone to help me."

I awkwardly hefted my body off the floor and leaned against the wall for support. I was shaking internally, even though I knew I wasn't hurt. Ever since the accident, any physical assault to my body elicited this response—I couldn't help it. But I was learning to separate myself from this reaction. I took a deep breath and talked myself through it. *You'll be okay. You'll be okay.* I took the towels and toiletries from Luke as he handed me each one and refilled the tote and then placed the metal pylon in the bag, too. I kept breathing through my tears while I scanned the sterile, white hallway for someone to help me.

Another mom and her young child from our swim class, freshly showered, were walking down the hall toward us. With watery, somewhat-embarrassed eyes, I caught her attention.

"Excuse me," I called. "My leg just broke. Can I get a hand?"

She looked down at my leg and I saw understanding register in her eyes. "Oh, of course. What can I do?"

I showed her how to hold her arm so she could support me as I hopped the two hundred feet down the rest of the hallway and into the parking lot to my car. She offered to carry my bag.

"I really appreciate your help," I said through my labored breath. Sweat was dripping down my brow by now because of the effort of jumping on one leg.

"Well, I think you're doing great. Is there anything else I can do?" We had arrived at the car.

"No, thanks, that was very helpful. Thank you." With shaky hands, I managed to get Luke secured into his car seat. I hopped around to my side of the car and slipped into my seat. After buckling myself in, I took a deep breath. *It's okay, you're fine. You can do this.*

On the drive home, I reminded myself to keep breathing and focus on the road. Luke started talking about Woody and Buzz Lightyear from *Toy Story*, his current favorite movie, which distracted me from my body's trembling. When we arrived home, I had to hop fifty more feet to the house, using the fence for support with one hand, supporting the baby in my belly with my other hand. In my younger Super Girl days, hopping up and down a flight of thirteen steps would have been a breeze. But now, after three years of relative inactivity—and being six months pregnant—I was exhausted by the effort. I fell onto the couch, and finally, a sob heaved out of me. I felt momentarily overwhelmed with what I'd just been through. But in only a few minutes, a realization crept into my heart and a slight smile onto my lips: I got through it. My leg had broken and fallen off my pregnant body in a public place while my little son stood beside me. And I got through it. I was handling everything I needed to handle.

Pregnancy for me was different than it was for other women. While some women jogged up until two weeks before they gave birth, I was taking care of a toddler while using a peg leg and increasingly losing physical ability with every pound I gained. That was just who I was. I sat on the couch, filled with the warmth of acceptance. I finally really understood that I had a choice in how I responded to each moment of my life. I didn't love my situation, but I acknowledged it as my own. My body might have been falling apart, but I was glad to know my spirit wasn't.

I settled Luke on the couch with a snack and a movie and then called Mark to tell him what happened.

"Do you need me to come home?" he said with some urgency.

Surprising myself, I said, "No, I'm fine, really, just a little bruised. I just needed to hear your voice, that's all." Hearing his velvety voice grounded me. "I'll call Kirk and make an appointment for tomorrow. Do you think you could take a few hours off work to come with me?" Technically, I could have crutched from the house to the car and from the car to the office, but with a toddler and my overstuffed mommy purse, it would be challenging on crutches. I didn't have anything to prove. I knew when to ask for help.

"Of course. Just let me know when."

Many men feel at a loss when their wives are pregnant and miserable. Not Mark. He was always there for me, ready to do what he could to make things easier. And my growing acceptance of my disability seemed to shift Mark's emotional response to me, and to help him relax into the experience of getting ready for a new baby, too. I was so grateful that instead of shoving him away with my anger, as I had during the first pregnancy, I was allowing him to support me, physically and emotionally.

By the eighth month of pregnancy, I was using my body in a very limited fashion: within the house and around the neighborhood. Looking after a toddler meant I sat on the floor a lot, which I've never liked. Getting back to standing was hard, especially as the baby grew. I would discover later that floor-sitting during pregnancy, when my pelvic region was shifting and changing, was the beginning of tendonitis in my sacrum, or "butt bone." But the domain of dinosaurs and superheroes is on the floor, so down I went. Life was slow until the baby arrived, and I was accepting. I had learned from my herbal medicine teacher to always ask of my pain, "What's right about this?" I posed the same question to my situation. Slowing down meant I was able to savor my moments with Luke. Slowing down meant I was able to honor my body. Slowing down meant I was able to protect my baby.

Mark and I consulted with a midwife and felt confident in having a home birth for my second delivery. When the day came, my sister Mary Beth and her eleven-year-old daughter, Mora, arrived in the wee hours of the morning to help out. While they tended to the chores, I labored through each contraction, fearful this birthing experience would be similar to the last: long and arduous. The midwife had assured me that labor would be quicker the second time around, but I had my doubts. She turned out to be right. This labor was half as long as Luke's.

I didn't want to be on my back again for the actual birth, so we rented a birthing tub, which was like a large heated kiddie pool. I was in the tub when I was ready to push, Mark behind me once again, helping my body move into each contraction. I started to cry, scared the pushing phase would last three hours as it had with Luke. But the baby wanted to come out. In just eighteen minutes, I pushed out my baby girl, Tessa.

She was tiny and pink, and when the midwife handed her to me I gasped at the blast of her red hair. Mark stood beside me once we'd swaddled her in a blanket, and the midwife invited Luke to come meet his baby sister. I watched him tentatively reach out to stroke her cheek. My little family.

An hour later, when we were in bed together, Tessa nursing contentedly, I looked down into her eyes. *Are you the other one? Did you come back to me?* I won't know until I am dead whether there is a world beyond this where aborted children's souls wait for their mommies to be ready for them, but I desperately hope there is. Tessa's deep-blue eyes looked up at me knowingly, and I decided her answer was yes.

24

• • •

TRULY SOMETHING SPECIAL

Mothering Tessa was a sweet experience. I loved her light, fairylike energy, loved watching Luke make sense of her presence, and loved knowing that my little family was complete. By the time Tessa was three, we were living in Bellingham, nearly two hours from Lynn, who had been so important in my healing over the years. I continued to drive down to see her on an as-needed basis. She'd kept me grounded for so long, and I sometimes still needed to hear her affirming mantras: Ride it out. Just breathe. I am whole.

During my visit to see her in December 2003 I talked to her about my desire to commemorate the upcoming twenty-fifth anniversary of my accident. Years ago, shortly after I'd met with Harvey, she had encouraged me to celebrate the anniversary of the accident as if it were a second birthday. Instead of latching onto morose feelings about the accident every winter, she wanted me to think of the date as the beginning of a new self—which it most certainly had been. So on the sixteenth anniversary, I'd started a new tradition: I went to the store and bought myself the prettiest cake I could find. When I first started this tradition, I was still single. Then Mark entered my life and though he wasn't a big cake eater, he understood the annual ceremony and indulged with me. As Luke and Tessa joined our lives, they joined me in loving this tradition, too, especially when I served the cake a la mode.

But I needed to commemorate the twenty-fifth anniversary with more than just cake. I was a completely changed woman from the girl I'd been when I first lost my leg. My healing had taken nearly a quarter of a century. And although I knew there would always be situations that would hook into my trauma, I also knew that I was over a hump I once thought I could never conquer. I was a grown, centered woman with two small children living a life that I had well in hand most days. Not perfect, but good. I needed to acknowledge the time I'd put in to get here. And I wanted Lynn to be a part of that because she had been my mentor and cheerleader along the often-rocky trail.

Lynn offered to drive up to Bellingham and share in a ritual with me that she would design especially for the occasion. I agreed whole-heartedly, and with blind faith. I had no idea what she had up her sleeve. I realized this went outside the traditional boundaries of a typical patient/therapist relationship, but I had been through a lot with Lynn and appreciated her offer. I trusted her implicitly and said, "Yes!"

Lynn couldn't make it up to Bellingham until the third week of the month, so my family and I still enjoyed my store-bought cake on January 3rd, the actual anniversary. And then on January 25th, Lynn drove up in her van and we met at a Park and Ride at the south end of town. She opened the back doors of her van to reveal a bright bouquet of helium balloons. Lynn dug into her purse and fumbled around until she found what she wanted. "Here it is," she said with enthusiasm. She pulled a black Sharpie pen from her purse and held it up like a torch. She invited me to sit in the back of her van.

I looked around me at the cars scattered around the parking lot, wondering if we were going to do our ritual right here. "What are we up to?" I asked.

She just smiled. "I want you to take this pen and write positive statements about how you are going to walk into your life from here on out," she instructed. "Don't worry, I've got a plan."

I tentatively took the pen from her, unsure at first of what to write. *Just breathe*, I said to myself. I knew how to listen to my heart by now. I knew that when I relaxed into the moment, words would come flooding in. And they did. I grabbed the bright-red balloon and wrote my first "Walking into Life" statement. Then I handed the balloon to Lynn for her to hold. Next I reached for the blue balloon and repeated the process. Lynn grinned as she took the balloon from me and saw what I'd written. Next was the yellow balloon and then the kelly green one. I wrote what came to mind without hesitation. "Great," Lynn said, when I handed her each of them. "What else?" I had one more statement to write. I took the orange balloon and closed my eyes to wait for the right statement to come to me. When it did, I printed it in large letters and handed the balloon to Lynn. She nodded, satisfied.

I watched as Lynn stuffed the balloon bouquet into the backseat of my Geo Prizm and instructed me to sit in the passenger's seat. I did as I was told and waited to see what was next. After we buckled in, I handed her the keys and Lynn started driving. As we drove south on the freeway, through hills covered with fir trees and the bare deciduous trees of deep winter, Lynn explained what we were going to do, "We'll drive beyond the site of your accident and then turn around so we're on the north side of the road. When we start driving by the section of freeway where your accident happened, I want you to take each balloon, one by one. Read the message you wrote out loud and then release the balloon out your window. Let's send your intentions flying, shall we?"

Before long she exited from the freeway south of the accident site, drove over the freeway and took the northbound on-ramp.

I unrolled my window and the balloons jumbled around in the backseat like a pile of leaves in a windstorm. The skin on my neck prickled not with fear, as had been the case many times on this stretch of road, but with excitement. I reached behind me and grabbed the closest balloon.

"Here's to Walking into Life, Colleen," Lynn said. "Read it like you mean it."

Kelly green balloon in hand, I read what I'd written on it and called out:

"My beauty is about who I am on the inside."

I stuck my hand out the window, clutching onto the ribbon attached to the kelly green balloon and then let go. The balloon frantically whipped away from me and then started slowly soaring up to the treetops. "Woohoo! " Lynn shouted above the din of air rushing into the car and the balloons hitting against each other in the backseat. "Grab another one." I reached into the backseat and grabbed the yellow balloon.

"This is my life's work, to become me," I shouted. I stuck my hand out the window and let go. Another intention soaring to the sky.

"I walk into my life with courage and joy." The red balloon floated up and away.

"I accept and love my body as it is." I felt the truth of this as I belted out the words and watched the blue balloon be taken by the wind.

Lynn whooped and hollered after each balloon.

And then I reached for the last balloon, the orange one. When I had the ribbon in my hand, I kissed the balloon for emphasis, held it out the window and yelled loudly:

"I am stepping into my wholeness." After I released that balloon, I started cheering right along with Lynn. She unrolled her window and then leaned on the horn and sent out a blast of shouts from the car.

We shouted and hooted with joy and declarations all the way back into town.

After twenty-five years, I was, truly, Walking into Life.

I didn't see Lynn much after that. She had been my partner in healing for so many years, but after that ritual I felt confident that I could figure my life out on my own.

Two years passed. Luke was eight and Tessa was five. Life marched on the way it should with school-age children: busily and happily.

January rolled around again and I bought a cake as I always did. Ever since Harvey and I had connected in Victoria after the fifteenth anniversary of the accident, he'd called me every year. We didn't often talk about the accident; we mostly caught up on each other's lives. When he called this year, I could hear in his voice that he was hurting. As our conversation was winding down, he blurted out, "I'd give you my leg if I could, Colleen." I had heard him say this before many times and, just like every other time, Harvey's guilt was palpable. As he said it this year, I wanted to reach through the phone line and hold his hand and assure him I was okay. I wanted to give him permission to be okay, too. *Maybe if he saw how well I'm doing, he would feel better*, I thought.

"Harvey, do you want to see each other again?" He did. We agreed to meet, but I insisted that this time we meet on my turf. I wanted him to see more than just my physical self. I wanted him to see my life.

Harvey was hesitant, "Oh, Colleen, I'm pretty tight these days. A hotel room isn't in my budget right now." He had already explained to me about being on a short-term disability leave from work.

Without thinking about it, I blurted out, "That's okay, you can stay with us."

"Really? That wouldn't be an inconvenience?" he asked.

"Not at all," I assured him. In fact I felt like it was just what he might need.

"But I've never driven that part of I-5 since the accident. I don't know if I can," he said, revealing just how vulnerable he felt. "Maybe I can find someone to drive me."

I hoped he would.

Sure enough, within a week, Harvey had found a friend who was driving to Seattle in a few weeks and could drop him off in Bellingham on the way south. Harvey would stay with us for two nights before his friend picked him up and took him home.

I was well aware that inviting the man responsible for the loss of my leg to stay at my house was unconventional, but I had learned to trust my instincts. Every cell in my body was telling me that Harvey and I needed to see each other again. I felt strongly that Harvey needed to come to me this time and if that meant staying at my house, then so be it. I trusted that this was the right decision.

The day before he arrived, after the kids went to school, I rolled up my sleeves and got out my cleaning supplies. I was compelled to clean my house top to bottom. The event that had changed my life was something I considered sacred now, and welcoming Harvey into my home felt like a holy act. I cleansed the house as if purifying a temple for a sanctified guest.

I thought this visit was to help relieve Harvey of his guilt, and perhaps it would help with that, but as I cleaned I came to understand that this visit was peeling away another layer of the onion for me, too. Throughout the day I thought about my journey since the accident. In reflection, I realized that I didn't focus so much on why this happened to me anymore. I understood that living the answer was more important than finding a concrete, stagnant answer. The meaning of my experiences would change and morph over time. What became as clear as my freshly polished coffee table was that my attitude and response to adversity mattered more than anything. I knew I would continue to walk through life with anger and sadness as my companions, but as I scoured the house, I also released my negative judgments about that. While I cleaned the bathroom mirror, I saw with crystal clarity that I lived inside the paradox of life. I understood that joy and sadness could coexist in the same moment. And I hoped Harvey would see that reflected in me.

The next day I put clean sheets on Luke's bed so Harvey could sleep in his room. I made some scones and readied a pot of tea. I prepared a place at my table for him as I had a number of years ago when I invited my sadness to the table.

Harvey arrived in the late afternoon while my kids were still in school. We drank the tea and ate the scones at the kitchen table and talked about how we were going to spend our time together. I said what had been brewing in my mind during my preparations,

"Harvey, I think it's time you went to the site of the accident. By avoiding it all these years, you've given it a lot of power."

"I know you're right. I've thought so, too," he said as he wrung his hands.

"It'll be okay. We'll do this together," I assured him. We decided that we would go the next day after I dropped the kids at school.

That night Harvey took all of us out to dinner and then taught us a fun card game as we sat around the kitchen table. My children accepted him without judgment or criticism. He was mommy's friend. That's all.

After the kids went to school the next morning, Harvey and I got in the car. Harvey, an avid hockey fan distracted himself as we drove through town to the freeway entrance by explaining some of the rules of the game. I was only half listening. I was distracted by the power of what we were about to do. Once I merged onto the freeway, Harvey stopped talking. He could tell this was too momentous for idle chatter. A heavy silence filled the car. I started sweating and shivering as I drove seven miles south. I could feel Harvey's anxiety build beside me, too.

I exited at the same place I had with Lynn two years before, drove over the overpass and turned left onto the northbound on-ramp. There were no other cars around, so I stopped the car before getting onto the freeway. I pointed, "So there's a speed limit sign up there about half a mile, see it?" Harvey looked ahead and nodded his head. "The accident happened just before that. I'll pull over when we get there, okay?"

"Okay," he said. My throat ached, and my eyes started watering. This was important; I could feel it in my cells. I had driven this stretch of the road hundreds of times. In order to protect my heart, I had to develop distance from the feelings that were essentially left on the roadway. Harvey had just kept his distance by never returning. And now, here we were together, going to the place where our souls met. And we weren't just going to drive past it; we were going to pause and linger there, to really *be* there.

I drove the half mile to the accident site and pulled over to the shoulder on the right-hand side of the freeway, which abutted a hillside. The cars rushing past us created a din and my car rattled as the semitrucks passed by. I pointed to the guardrail on the left shoulder of the freeway. "See that dent there? That's where it happened." Harvey let out a sob. And then another. He couldn't stop. His big shoulders drooped and shook as he let out twenty-seven years of pent-up sorrow. I cried right along with him.

I reached into my coat pocket and pulled out a tissue for each of us. Harvey grabbed his tissue and my sweaty hand. We held hands and looked out the window at the dent in the guardrail; and we cried. "If I could give you my leg, I would," he said once again.

I looked at him directly and wiped my tears. "Harvey, I don't want your leg—or anyone's leg. I am full and complete the way I am. I am okay."

He looked up at me with hope in his eyes.

"Really," I said as I squeezed his hand. I looked over at the guardrail again. "This is just a spot on the planet, but it's our spot. And we're okay, Harvey. We're both okay."

"This is crazy. I can't believe we're here together," he said through his tears.

"Yeah, this is ludicrous, isn't it?" I replied, through my own tears.

I looked at him and he looked at me. Before we knew it, we both started laughing. Deep, hard belly laughs. We laughed with the realization that in that moment we could release our mutual pain. We were both there together, insanely justified in our existence. We didn't necessarily know where we were going from there, but in that moment, we understood how absurd and genuinely powerful life could be. We laughed until our bellies ached and our cheeks hurt.

I was acutely aware of the sound of my car rattling as the cars and trucks passed us at sixty miles an hour; eventually, I felt we'd faced danger enough for one day. I couldn't sit idle on the side of the freeway any longer. I had learned to normalize my fears by honoring my needs. I turned on the car and got us home safely.

After Harvey left the next morning, I took a slow walk around the neighborhood, but instead of walking, I felt like I was floating on the waves of the sea cresting at the shore's edge. Waves of insights crashed over me. Through hard work and intentionality, I had shifted my focus from what I had lost to what I had gained. I didn't just survive my injury; I had put my arms around it and made something of it for me and my family—and maybe for Harvey, too. I understood that I had found something with more meaning than my loss: acceptance and love. I had been aching my whole life to be someone special. It turns out, I always had been that someone.

EPILOGUE

I had wanted to take my kids backpacking ever since Luke was born, but I wasn't ready until Luke was ten and Tessa was seven. A friend recommended a "one-mile flat trail" to a beautiful lake in the North Cascades. *I can do a mile*, I thought. That's walking to school and back. My friend loaned us some backpacks for the kids, and Mark and I bought a couple of two-man tents, one for the boys and one for the girls.

The drive to the trailhead took longer than we expected, so it was after two p.m. when we parked and got our hiking boots on.

Entering the trail from the parking lot was like stepping into a different world. Suddenly, we were enveloped in green of all kinds: the dark green of the fir needles, the chartreuse of the Solomon's seal, the deep waxy green of salal, the bright kelly green of bunchberry. The clean, musky smell of pine trees encircled me. We walked along the beginning of the trail, and I wanted to weep with joy to be back amid this beauty. I was among long-lost friends.

At first, the trail was flat and relatively easy. After about a quarter mile, I found my stride and became used to the weight of the back-pack. Then the trail became a maze of roots lying just on the surface. I kept my head down, deliberately placing each step. I walked slowly to avoid a fall and to soak in this emerald paradise.

We came upon some steps built into the trail by a work crew. They were well made but steep and unexpected. After the steps, the trail evened out, then rose. And then the trail presented more steps. Mark was there for each one. He was a step ahead of me and offered his hand to help pull me up. Ten steps, then trail; five steps, more trail; twelve steps, more trail. They just didn't stop. My knee started to ache.

Luke walked quickly up the trail and was soon too far ahead of us to hear our calls. Mark took off his pack and ran ahead to find him. Luke, still looking fresh as a daisy, walked back to where Tessa and I were waiting. I could see he had plenty of energy to expel, but we needed to be able to keep track of him.

"Luke, I know it's fun to run ahead, but stay within earshot, okay?" I pleaded.

"*Okay*," he said, rolling his eyes. We continued the hike.

When I was sure we had walked a mile, I looked for a sign pointing us to a campsite. But there was no sign yet. Only more steps, more trail. *Didn't my friend say this was a flat trail?* I wondered if we took the wrong one. The ache in my knee increased to stabbing pains, which pierced my knee with each stair I climbed. I started to think the hike hadn't been such a good idea after all.

"Maybe we should go back, Mark. This is really hurting. I don't know how I'll get back down tomorrow if my knee is hurt or swollen."

"Why don't you take off your pack and leave it by the trail, honey. I'll come back and get it once we've found a campsite. Carrying less weight may make the steps easier."

I agreed and laid my pack by the side of the trail. I continued climbing the stairs. Mark was right; walking was much easier without the added weight. I asked Mark to go ahead with the kids and find out how much farther camp was. More steps, more trail.

A dad and his two children came down the trail. I didn't bother with niceties. I just cut to the chase.

"How much farther?" I asked through labored breath, trying not to sound desperate.

"Oh, you're almost there. It's a beautiful lake," he said.

Almost there. I became filled with emotion so intense I had to stop and soak in the beauty of the moment. *I've almost done it.* This trail was one of the most beautiful trails I'd ever been on, perhaps because I didn't know if it would be my last. I looked around with such gratitude that my body had brought me here. I was so thankful to be in the forest again. I was so aware that this moment would never come my way again, even if I did hike another trail in my lifetime. This moment was all I wanted.

After another slow quarter mile, the last step reunited me with my family. We found a stunning camping spot high above the lake, nestled in ripe blueberry bushes. While Mark went down trail to retrieve my backpack, the kids and I started unloading their packs and setting up camp.

Luke had difficulty making the transition to his new, wild environment. Suddenly his bounding energy waned.

"Mom, I'm tired. That was too much walking. And there's nothing to do up here. I'm bored."

"Luke we just got here. How can you be bored?"

"Well, look around, there's nothing to do," he whined.

"We have to set up our tents. Come on, buddy, I need your help figuring these out."

But Luke wouldn't be swayed. He couldn't believe he was suddenly thrust into this green world devoid of any games, screens, toys, or trading cards. His whining didn't let up, and I felt a wave of annoyance and resentment. I had just finished the hike of my life with my husband and children—one I'd dreamed about taking for years—and now one of my children was tainting the fresh mountain air with his griping. "Luke, enough!" I said firmly.

He stormed off into the nearby bushes and sat his anger off on a log. Tessa and I figured out how to set up the girl tent and began picking blueberries. *Plunk, plunk, plunk*, they each said, as they landed in the metal pot. A family of crows cawed from a nearby tree, making a ruckus. I looked up and smiled, remembering how I'd loved cawing back to the crows when I was a girl. "Caw, caw, caw," I bellowed. "Caw, caw, caw," Tessa joined. And, just like when I was a girl, the crows became silent and seemed perplexed. I chuckled and we continued picking blueberries.

When Mark returned with my backpack, it was time to make dinner. Luke slowly emerged from the bushes and went to the stream with Mark to get water. When dinner was ready, Luke's mood had shifted and he was engaged with us again. Before we ate our meal we held hands, just like we do before dinner at home, and said our "happys." This is a time to reflect on something about the day that we are each grateful for. I'd spent many years wanting to recreate the kind of family I had as a child, but sitting under the trees listening to my little family express their gratitude made me swell with pride. I had long ago let go of having the perfect husband, the perfect children, the perfect anything. One of my biggest lessons was that no one and nothing is perfect. We are all beautifully flawed.

The next morning, as the sun crested over the eastern peaks, we walked down to the lake. The mountains surrounding the lake were mirrored in the placid surface, a tableau so exquisite, my heart nearly burst. *It's been so long.* Mark and the kids climbed onto a huge logjam at the southern end of the lake. I crawled out onto the jam as far as I could, found a comfy log, soaked in the sun, and took pictures of my family. I was in heaven.

We headed back to the campsite, packed up the tents and other gear, and headed back to the trail. I lingered for a few moments and allowed the beauty to envelope me. I took a deep breath. This moment was not just this moment; it held every spark of inspiration nature had ever provided me, from my first backpacking trip as a teenager with two legs, to this moment now. I stood in awe, bowed my head in gratitude, and whispered, "Thank you."

Mark and Tessa took the lead this time. Without prompting, Luke stayed behind. The trail started out with descending steps. At the first stair, I looked up to see Luke standing on the step below, holding out his hand.

"Here, Mom, let me help you."

"Oh, thanks, buddy." I took his big, strong, ten-year-old hand and stepped down, bearing my weight onto his hand. He supported me. All the way down the trail.

READER'S GUIDE

• ● •

QUESTIONS FOR DISCUSSION

1. After the accident, Colleen's faith is tested while she grieves for her leg and for the girl she once was. She finds that her faith isn't the balm and safety net that it was after her father died. Why do you think that is?

2. One of Colleen's conflicts centers around her identity. As she adjusts to a life as an amputee, she gets that sense from some people that she is inspirational, but from other people she gets the message that she must carry on like nothing happened. Can you give examples from the story that created this conflict?

3. What do you think of the thank-you notes that Colleen's mother expects her to write to people who send flowers and casseroles while Colleen is in the hospital? What do you think of Colleen's need to comply? When do you think family and social conventions should take a backseat?

4. *A Leg to Stand On* offers clear descriptions of the challenges of living life on one leg. Has reading this book given you a different perspective on the life of an amputee? If so, in what way?

5. Even in the midst of her big family, Colleen experiences loneliness. She tries to find other amputees to commiserate with—but when she joins the ski group and the soccer team, she finds

that other amputees don't share her need to talk about the deep feelings brought on by her disability. Do they understand her? Where else in the book do you see this theme emerge?

6. Colleen recounts her experiences of having two abortions. How much does her disability play a role in her decisions? How does her faith play a role in her decisions?

7. Forgiveness is a theme that runs through both sections of this book. How does Colleen's childhood faith both help and hinder her ability to forgive Harvey? To forgive herself for her abortions?

8. The first thing Colleen does after she is sure she will go through with her third pregnancy is call her mother. This ties the reader all the way back to the prologue—Colleen's belief in the importance of family and her desire to have children. Why do you think she feels such a need to call her mother to tell her about this pregnancy when she felt she could not tell her about the abortions?

9. What do you think of the advice Colleen receives from Lynn— that she isn't responsible to the children who asked questions about her prosthetic leg? Do you remember a time when you were a young child or a parent of a young child and you saw someone with a disability in public? How did you feel as a child? Did it scare you or intrigue you? What did you do? If you are a parent, how did you explain that person's disability to your child?

10. In the last chapter, when Colleen takes Harvey to the site of the accident, she says to him, "Harvey, I don't want your leg. I'm full and complete the way I am." When do you see Colleen's shift from viewing her missing leg as a hole in her life to feeling whole without it? In what areas in your life do you feel like you are missing something? Where are you on the acceptance continuum in accepting these losses?

ACKNOWLEDGMENTS

This book has taken me many years to write. They say we don't write alone, and although I felt alone when I woke up at five thirty every morning to fit my writing around my family's busy schedule, the truth of the matter is, I have been blessed to have had a slew of people supporting me, cheering me on, and encouraging me to continue to write.

That you have made my life complete is an understatement. Mark, Luke, and Tessa, you have brought a depth of joy and love to my life that I didn't know existed until you joined me on this journey. Thank you.

I am blessed and privileged to have been born into the Haggerty clan. Growing up, we were eight strong. We have since grown to twenty-six. Thanks to each of you for all the love, laughter, and support: Mom, Dad, Larry, Maureen, Tom, Katie, Mary Beth, Bill, Liam, Mora, Kevin, Molly, Brendon, Patrick, Lara Rose, Matthew, Marc, David, Meg, Reed, Abby, Matthew, and Andrew.

Harvey, there are no words. I send you a hug.

My soul has been sheltered and sustained, protected and nourished by my female friends. Deep gratitude to my "oaks," Sue, Margi, Sandra, Ceci, and Laurel.

The therapist in the book is a compilation of two women that supported me when I was in my late twenties and early thirties:

Anne and Ana (see, it would have been confusing). I hope it's clear how much they helped me. My gratitude to them runs deep.

Thanks to my Possibility Posse—Penny, Pat, Lori, and Dennis—for your support and encouragement during the years it took me to write this book. And Pat, I appreciate the use of your cabin so I could retreat from life and sink into the memories.

A shout out of thanks to my writing group—Jackie, Stephanie, Carol and Blanche—for their enthusiastic support during the process of birthing my book.

Ann Weinstock, thank you for creating the perfect cover.

Laura Kalpakian, I am indebted to you for everything I learned from you during your nine-month memoir writing class. You inspired me to move beyond the essay and into a full-fledged book.

Merrik Bush Pirkle, my first editor, thank you for bringing new vision to my book and handling the material tenderly.

Cami Ostman, editor extraordinaire, brought wise insight to the arc of the book and helped me reshape it. Thank you for your masterful untangling and your refreshing viewpoints.

Brooke Warner has been with me since I started this book. She was the one who shone a flashlight when I went into the dark places. She is a true guide, an inspirational mentor, and an intuitive, encouraging, partner. You have my deepest thanks.

Not only did this book take many years to write, the story itself spans many years. They say no one is an island, and although I spent much of my life feeling isolated and alone, the truth of the matter is, since I lost my leg, I have been blessed to have had teachers, friends, and strangers tucked into key moments of my life who have reminded me with heartbreaking clarity how truly connected we all are. There are too many of you to mention, but if you read this book because of your personal connection to me, you are one of those people. Thank you for being a part of my community.

ABOUT THE AUTHOR

• ● •

© Kaila Williams

Colleen Haggerty is a writer of memoir and personal essay. She has contributed to four anthologies: *The Spirit of a Woman*, *He Said What?* (penned as Colleen Robinson*), Dancing at the Shame Prom*, and *Beyond Belief*. After Colleen lost her leg at seventeen years old she found herself feeling marginalized. She developed a deep empathy for and desire to help others living on the fringe of society, which led to her twenty year career in non-profit management. Mentoring others is a way of life for Colleen and was especially true when she worked as executive director for Big Brothers Big Sisters of Northwest Washington. She is an inspiring public speaker and was a speaker at the 2013 Bellingham TEDx event where she talked about the power of forgiveness. She is an avid collager and, as a cancer survivor herself, facilitates SoulCollage™ workshops at the local cancer center. Colleen writes about walking through life as an amputee at www.colleenhaggerty.com. She makes her home in Bellingham, WA with her husband and two teenagers.

SELECTED TITLES FROM SHE WRITES PRESS

She Writes Press is an independent publishing company
founded to serve women writers everywhere.
Visit us at www.shewritespress.com.

Americashire: A Field Guide to a Marriage by Jennifer Richardson
$15.95, 978-1-938314-30-8
A couple's decision about whether or not to have a child plays out against
the backdrop of their new home in the English countryside.

Splitting the Difference: A Heart-Shaped Memoir by Tré Miller-Rodríguez
$19.95, 978-1-938314-20-9
When 34-year-old Tré Miller-Rodríguez's husband dies suddenly from a
heart attack, her grief sends her on an unexpected journey that culminates
in a reunion with the biological daughter she gave up at 18.

Green Nails and Other Acts of Rebellion: Life After Loss by Elaine Soloway
$16.95, 978-1-63152-919-1
An honest, often humorous account of the joys and pains of caregiving for
a loved one with a debilitating illness.

Where Have I Been All My Life? A Journey Toward Love and Wholeness
by Cheryl Rice
$16.95, 978-1-63152-917-7
Rice's universally relatable story of how her mother's sudden death
launched her on a journey into the deepest parts of grief—and, ultimately,
toward love and wholeness.

Breathe: A Memoir of Motherhood, Grief, and Family Conflict by Kelly Kittel
$16.95, 978-1-938314-78-0
A mother's heartbreaking account of losing two sons in the span of nine
months—and learning, despite all the obstacles in her way, to find joy in
life again.

Seeing Red: A Woman's Quest for Truth, Power, and the Sacred by Lone Morch
$16.95, 978-1-938314-12-4
One woman's journey over inner and outer mountains—a quest that takes
her to the holy Mt. Kailas in Tibet, through a seven-year marriage, and
into the arms of the fierce goddess Kali, where she discovers her powerful,
feminine self.

CPSIA information can be obtained
at www.ICGtesting.com
Printed in the USA
FSOW01n0735301014
3336FS